Introduction to Financial Accounting

University of Illinois Urbana Champaign Edition

Cunningham / Nikolai / Bazley

CENGAGE
Learning·

Australia • Brazil • Japan • Korea • Mexico • Singapore • Spain • United Kingdom • United States

**Introduction to Financial Accounting
University of Illinois Urbana Champaign
Edition
Cunningham / Nikolai / Bazley**

Senior Project Development Manager:
 Linda deStefano

Marketing Specialist:
 Courtney Sheldon

Senior Production/Manufacturing Manager:
 Donna M. Brown

Production Editorial Manager:
 Kim Fry

Sr. Rights Acquisition Account Manager:
 Todd Osborne

For product information and technology assistance, contact us at
Cengage Learning Customer & Sales Support, 1-800-354-9706

For permission to use material from this text or product,
submit all requests online at **cengage.com/permissions**
Further permissions questions can be emailed to
permissionrequest@cengage.com

Compilation © 2013 Cengage Learning

ISBN-13: 978-1-285-88492-9

ISBN-10: 1-285-88492-2

Cengage Learning
5191 Natorp Boulevard
Mason, Ohio 45040
USA

Cengage Learning is a leading provider of customized learning solutions with office locations around the globe, including Singapore, the United Kingdom, Australia, Mexico, Brazil, and Japan. Locate your local office at:
international.cengage.com/region.
Cengage Learning products are represented in Canada by Nelson Education, Ltd.
For your lifelong learning solutions, visit **custom.cengage.com.**
Visit our corporate website at **cengage.com.**

Printed in the United States of America

Dear Students:

There is a saying that "knowledge is power." But for that to be true, knowledge must be based on an objective, independent thought process that tests new information against evidence, assumptions, bias, and other points of view. In other words, in order for you to gain new "knowledge," you must "think through" the related issues and ideas, understand them, satisfy yourself that they are reasonable, and make them a part of your personal knowledge base. Furthermore, you must be willing to re-evaluate that knowledge, and perhaps change it, as new issues and ideas arise.

In business, the saying is true—knowledge *is* power. Those who have it hold a competitive advantage over those who don't. Those who understand the business information, and know how to interpret and use it, make the best business decisions.

A company's accounting reports, generated by its integrated accounting system, are a major source of business information. But when reading these reports, you must evaluate the information they contain by looking for supporting evidence, assumptions, and bias, and by considering other points of view. Furthermore, you must know how to *interpret* the information contained in these reports. To do this, you must understand how a company's integrated accounting system develops these reports, and what concepts, principles, and assumptions underlie the accounting information contained in these reports. With this in mind, we designed this book to address all of these issues.

After you graduate, you may work for a company and use its accounting information to make decisions as an "internal user." Or, you may consider investing in a company, or have some other reason to use its accounting information to make decisions as an "external user." Your ability to use the material in this book later to help you make effective business decisions (regardless of your career choice) depends on your making it a part of your own knowledge base. This means that you should "think through" the issues and ideas as you read about them, making sure that you understand them before you read further. This will require some effort on your part. As you read the book, read it critically. Test it in your mind. Does it make sense to you?

To help you learn this material and think about what you are learning, we have placed questions throughout the book, labeled with a "stop light," that we think are worth your time and effort to answer. Each time you encounter one of these questions, stop, think through the question, and answer it honestly. Base your answer on what you have learned in your life experiences, on your knowledge of accounting, business, and the world, and on your own common sense. By pausing in your reading and answering these questions, you will have time to process what you are reading and an opportunity to build new knowledge into your already-existing knowledge base.

Besides answering these questions as you read the book, think about what questions you have, or what else you would like to know about the subject at hand. Pursuing the answers to these questions, in class or otherwise, will help you add to your knowledge base and the quality of your later decisions.

We hope you find this book interesting and fun to read!! We also hope you find it useful in increasing your knowledge of accounting, your appreciation of the power of using accounting information for making business decisions, and your ability to use accounting information for your own business decisions.

BRIEF CONTENTS

CONTENTS

CHAPTER 3   **DEVELOPING A BUSINESS PLAN: BUDGETING 72**

PREFACE

CAUTION:

This textbook has a number of themes that revolve around candy, and this preface is no exception. While this book has a lot of the great accounting ingredients you are used to (and all that you will need), it also "breaks the mold" as it incorporates a number of phrases and terms well known to candy lovers (and we believe that includes accountants). Our intent is that you will get a number of cravings while reading this preface, not the least of which is the desire to devour this book and to share its great taste with your colleagues and your students.

Two Great Courses that Make One Great Text . . .

You may recall hearing different food or beverage products promoting how natural and good they are for you by using the phrases "No artificial colors. No artificial sweeteners." Well, we would like to paraphrase those slightly to convey a similar message that is the initial premise as to why this text for the elementary accounting sequence is natural and good for you: "No artificial separation!"

In the real world, today's students will face an accounting environment where management accounting and financial accounting issues are integrated every day. The traditional—and artificial—separation of these topics in textbooks, however, tends to lead students to a perception that the two areas are unrelated. We also believe that traditional and highly technical "preparer-oriented" accounting textbooks (1) isolate accounting from general business decisions, (2) lose students' interest, and (3) reinforce a common misconception that accounting is best left only to accountants. Therefore, such a separation misses the big picture of an integrated accounting system that provides economic information to all users—which is what the overwhelming majority of your students in introductory accounting will be. This textbook thoroughly integrates management accounting and financial accounting topics in a way that is more reflective of the world students will face outside of the classroom.

Sometimes You Feel Like a Debit, Sometimes You Don't . . .

A major focus of this textbook is on *using* management accounting and financial accounting information in various business settings. Therefore, we wrote this book at a "nontechnical" level for *all* business and nonbusiness students—not just those intending to be accounting majors. But, because two of us are heavily involved in teaching intermediate accounting and write an intermediate accounting textbook, we are also aware of the needs of your accounting majors. So we also discuss *accumulating* and *reporting* accounting information. We take a nonprocedural approach by explaining transactions in terms of the accounting equation (and entries into "account columns") and *the effect of these transactions on the financial statements* rather than in terms of debits and credits. But, we realize there is a need in many situations to teach procedures. To that end, we have provided a full chapter-length appendix (Appendix A) on recording, storing, summarizing, and reporting accounting information. This appendix covers the accounting cycle, from journal entries (using debits and credits) through the post-closing trial balance. We designed it so that you may use it anywhere you see fit in the process of teaching from this book. We assure you that our accounting majors who have used this elementary accounting text are well-prepared to enter our intermediate accounting classes.

Ingredients and Nutritional Information (Key Features of this Text)

An Introduction to Business Approach

Chapters 1 and 9 take an "introduction to business" approach to orient students to the business environment—that is, the operations of a company, the different functions of business, managers' responsibilities, and the types of information, management reports, and financial statements the company's integrated accounting system provides for use in internal and external decision making. These chapters provide students with a basic understanding of business so they can more effectively envision the context in which accounting information is collected and used, and the types of decisions users make in this context. This approach allows students to see the "big picture" more clearly.

Creative and Critical Thinking

A section in Chapter 1 introduces students to creative and critical thinking and demonstrates how they are used in decision making and problem solving. Both volumes of this book emphasize the type of analytical thinking that successful accountants and other business people use in a world that is constantly changing and becoming more complex. We believe that as you use analytical thinking in your decision process regarding this textbook, you will not only decide to adopt the book but will also be able to use it in a way that will foster your students' growth.

In keeping with the creative and critical thinking coverage, the remaining chapters introduce students to various aspects of accounting and are designed to help them develop their thinking skills. "STOP" questions throughout the textbook (identified by a "stop light") ask students to take a break from reading, and to think about an issue and/or consider the outcome of a situation. We also ask them *why* they think what they think. The end-of-chapter (EOC) materials include both structured and unstructured questions and problems that emphasize the use of creative and critical thinking skills by the students. Therefore, some of the questions and problems do not have a "correct" answer. The focus is on the approach or process that students use to solve them. With the increasing complexity of business activities, we think our inclusion of creative and critical thinking materials will better prepare students to understand the substantive issues involved in new or unusual business practices.

The Simpler Things

Earlier, we mentioned a "nontechnical" approach. Although we explain identifying, measuring, recording, and reporting of economic information, we discuss these activities at a basic level (increases and decreases in account balances) and do not include a discussion of debit and credit rules and journal entries in the main body of the text. We do emphasize the double-entry accounting system through the use of the accounting equation (Assets = Liabilities + Owners' Equity) and its linkage to the income equation (Income = Revenues − Expenses). We use account columns to record transactions, but we explain the increases or decreases in relation to the accounting equation, rather than as debits and credits. At the same time, we also emphasize the effects of the transactions on a company's financial statements and the impact they have on analysis of the company (e.g., its risk, liquidity, financial flexibility, operating capability). We chose this approach to better help students gain an understanding of the logic of the accounting system and its interrelationships, the effects of transactions on a company's financial statements, and the use of accounting information in decision making without getting them "bogged down" in the mechanics of the system. For those wanting to incorporate the mechanics of the system, as we mentioned earlier, we do provide a thorough coverage of debits, credits, and journal entries in Appendix A.

Because You've Kept Us Apart for Too Long...

We also mentioned earlier that both volumes of this book integrate management accounting and financial accounting topics in a way that is more reflective of the world students will face outside of the classroom. In blending our discussion of management accounting and financial accounting, we address several management accounting topics prior to discussing specific financial accounting topics. In large part, a company must plan its activities before it communicates its plans to external users, and it must operate and evaluate its operations (internal decision making) before it communicates the results of its operations to external users. Therefore, in keeping with the "introduction to business" theme and the logical sequencing of business activities, we discuss accounting for planning first, and then for operating and evaluating (controlling)—discussing management accounting and financial accounting where they logically fit into this framework.

For instance, Chapter 2 covers cost-profit-volume (CVP) analysis for planning purposes. After students have an understanding of cost and revenue relationships, we introduce them to budgeting in Chapter 3. The discussion of the master budget includes projected financial statements, which links the coverage back to the financial statements we mentioned in Chapter 1. Chapter 4 then introduces accounting for the operations of a company. Chapters 5 through 7 describe a company's major financial statements and discuss how external users would use these statements to analyze the company.

Besides integrating management accounting and financial accounting topics, both volumes of this book also integrate business issues and values and international issues, where appropriate. This approach reinforces the idea that societal and global issues are not topics that can and should be dealt with separately from the other issues, but rather are an integral and significant part of business in today's world.

Plain—and with Peanuts (Building Block Approach)

This textbook also uses a building-block approach. It begins with starting and operating a small retail candy store—a sole proprietorship—and then progresses through the operations of a more complex company in the form of a candy manufacturer—a corporation. This allows students to learn basic concepts first, and then later to broaden and reinforce those concepts in a more complex setting. Several of the same topics reemerge, but each time they are refined or enhanced by a different company structure, a different type of business, or a different user perspective. For example, because of its location at the beginning of the semester, the Chapter 2 discussion of CVP analysis is simple. We cover it again in greater depth in Chapter 10, after students have a better understanding of costs in a manufacturing setting. Each time we revisit an issue, we discuss the uses of accounting information for both internal and external decision making, as appropriate.

Likewise, we use a building-block approach to arranging the end-of-chapter materials according to levels of learning. To indicate these levels, we have divided the homework into sections on *Testing Your Knowledge, Applying Your Knowledge*, and *Making Evaluations*. These categories are arranged so that the answers to questions require students to use increasingly higher-order thinking skills as they move from one category of question to the next. The *Testing Your Knowledge* section includes questions that test students' knowledge of specifics—terminology, specific facts, concepts and principles, classifications, and so forth. The *Applying Your Knowledge* section includes questions, problems, and situations that test students' abilities to translate, interpret, extrapolate, and apply their knowledge. The *Making Evaluations* section includes questions, problems, and cases that not only test students' abilities to apply their knowledge but also their abilities to analyze elements, relationships, and principles, to synthesize a variety of information, and to make judgments based on evidence and accounting criteria.

New and Improved Flavor

In this third edition, as a result of our own use of the book and of feedback from other users, we have made both volumes of the book even better. These are the major changes and new features of the text.

1. We moved the major content of the creative and creative thinking material to Chapter 1 (from Chapter 2). This allows instructors to cover this material in conjunction with the overall discussion of business, accounting, and decision making, without devoting an entire chapter to the topic. We also moved up the relevant homework from Chapter 2.

2. We included a brief discussion of the *FASB Accounting Standards Codification*™ (FASB Codification) in Chapter 1 and updated the related discussion of the role of the SEC.

3. In the Appendix to Chapter 1, we added a discussion of the prevention and detection of fraud to the section describing management advisory services.

4. Companies continue to become more international in their business activities. As a result, we added an introductory discussion of international financial reporting standards (IFRS) to Chapter 1, and expanded this discussion in Chapter 9. Then, in Volume 2, we provide an elementary comparison of U.S. GAAP with IFRS in regard to inventory in Chapter 18, property and equipment (and intangibles) in Chapter 20, bonds and leases in Chapter 21, and stocks and earnings in Chapter 23.

5. In Chapter 19, we expanded the discussion of capital rationing so that it now includes a method for ranking potential investments in a capital rationing situation.

6. Because reporting of impairments has become more important in today's economy, we added a discussion of goodwill impairment in Chapter 20 and "other than temporary" impairments of investments in Chapter 21.

7. Because fair value is becoming more prominent in companies' financial statements, we added a discussion of fair value as it applies to bonds payable in Chapter 21 and investments in Chapter 22.

8. Because reporting of pension liabilities continues to be important in today's economy, we expanded the related discussion in Chapter 21.

9. To introduce students to the increasing issuance of "hybrid securities" by companies, we added an elementary discussion of convertible bonds to Chapter 21.

10. We revised the Summary Surfing sections in various chapters to update the internet homework.

11. We revised many "real" company examples in the text, and also updated the "real" company problems in the homework.

We believe these changes enhance the "flavor" of the book and make its topics even more relevant and understandable to our students.

Real-World/World-Wide/Total World:

Life is not a "textbook case." That's why we not only integrate management accounting and financial accounting topics, but also include information about real-world companies as examples for many of these topics. And, we include analyses of the financial information of some of these companies in the text and in the homework materials of many chapters. We also include a "Summary Surfing" section in each chapter that gives students the opportunity to connect to some of these companies via the Internet for further evaluation.

Because each company's Web site may provide a unique path to its financial information, and each organization's Web site will be unique from each other organization's Web site, we provide helpful "surfing" instructions in the following two sections. You may want to direct your students' attention to these sections.

Suggestions for Navigating (Surfing!) a Company's Web site:

Generally, you can access a company's home page by typing in the name of the company in place of "companyname" in the following generic Web address: http://www."companyname".com. If that fails, you can use a search engine, like Yahoo or Google, to locate the company's home page. After you have accessed a company's home page, you can locate its financial statements, annual reports, and other financial information by finding a link on the home page to "About Us," "Company," "Company Information," "Investors," "Investor Relations," "Investor Information", or some combination of these terms.

After clicking on this link, you will be sent to the company's financial information. Many times, you can click on the company's annual report for a specific year to find all of the company's financial statements, notes to its financial statements, and related information. Sometimes, however, the company will show a "condensed" annual report which contains only "summary" financial statements. In this case, if you want complete financial information about the company for a specific year, you will need to find the company's SEC 10-K report for that year. Normally, the company's Web site will reference its 10-K report by providing a link to "SEC Filings." To find the financial statements, after clicking on the link, go to Part 2, Item 8 of the 10-K report.

Suggestions for Navigating (Surfing!) an Organization's Web site:

Generally, you can access an organization's (e.g., AICPA) home page by typing in the name of the organization in place of "organizationname" in the following generic Web address: http://www."organizationname".org. If that fails, you can use a search engine, like Yahoo or Google, to locate the organization's home page. After you have accessed an organization's home page, you will have to search the heading or body of that page, the drop-down menus, or "hot links" for an "entry" into the section of the Web site that is likely to contain the information for which you are looking. You may find that you have to go down several "paths" before you find the proper section. Unfortunately, because organizations' Web sites tend to be less standardized than those of corporations, you may find yourself using the "trial and error" method of finding information on those Web sites.

Serving Suggestions (How to Use this Text)

". . . . a well thought out and very well-planned text. The explanations are easy to read and follow. I could teach myself from this book."
— Rebe Herling, Student

Since we (and others) have used this book in our classes, we thought you might appreciate hearing what we have learned from this experience:

1. **Faculty Preferences:** For years, Hershey's made the Kiss only in plain chocolate. Although they had put almonds in a chocolate bar, they couldn't perfect doing so with a Kiss. Nonetheless, they kept trying, and as you know, succeeded several years ago. It has been a great success since then. You, too, can succeed in integrating the financial and managerial accounting areas for the best taste. For financial accounting faculty, the textbook is so well written (see student quote above) that the management accounting material is not difficult to teach. For management accounting faculty, the book leads with management accounting material and contains fewer financial procedures than traditional ones do, so it is not difficult to teach either.

2. **The Transfer Issue:** The two volumes of this book do not form an Oreo cookie. They are not designed so that you can split up the parts and eat them separately. Given that most transfer students will check out the receiving school's policies first, we suggest that receiving schools using our book advise transfer students that they should take their entire accounting sequence at one school or the other, but not half and half. To sending schools using our book, we suggest you give your students similar advice. For your course sequence, we suggest that you devote sufficient time to coverage of Appendix A (the accounting cycle, including debits and credits) so that your students who transfer to another school have an adequate foundation in accounting procedures.

3. **Pedagogy:** We designed the pedagogical features of this book with the purpose of guiding the readers through it in a way that will help them learn the material in the book. Opening introductory questions for each chapter highlight the major topics and pique students' interest, as well as guide their reading. In support of these questions, as we mentioned earlier, "STOP" questions throughout each chapter ask students to pause and answer a question related to what they have just read, which primes them for what comes next.

Each question encourages reflection, critical thinking, and understanding while students read the chapter and helps them build on their previous experience while learning accounting. The Summary at the end of each chapter briefly answers the opening introductory questions, but it also encourages students to use their creative and critical thinking skills to expand on the key points of the chapter.

Each time we use the accounting equation and account columns in the text to show the effect of a transaction on a company's accounts, we accompany that illustration with a description of the effect of the transaction on the company's financial statements. A marginal box next to the equation details this effect on the components of each of the financial statements affected by the transaction.

We include the financial section of Colgate-Palmolive's annual report in Appendix B (in the second volume of the book). We have homework assignments at the ends of many chapters in Volume 2 that ask students questions about the financial information in this annual report.

4. **How to Use the End-of-Chapter Materials:** This book is constructed in a "building block" approach, and so is the homework. We suggest you assign it in the same manner: ask students to test their knowledge first, then apply their knowledge, and finally, after building a strong base of understanding, make evaluations. Each chapter has a Dr. Decisive problem that asks students to apply their new knowledge in a situation closer to one they might be currently experiencing, making accounting a little more personal and relevant for them. In a "Dear Abby" format, students are asked to answer a "problem" mailed in by a reader. We have found it to be a fun way for students to work on teams, where the team constructs an answer to the question or evaluates another team's answer to the question.

Dr. Decisive

5. **Snickers®:** . . . by chuckling at the joke, the accounting concept it illustrated was planted firmly in my mind." – Lisa Mitchell, Student. The cartoons and photographs in the book are not just for levity. They provide visual enhancements of ideas, as well as humor, and help students apply their knowledge by interpreting cartoons and photos.

6. **Smooth or Crunchy?** Alternative Course: We wrote this book for the elementary accounting sequence, but the very nature of its design has led to its successful use in MBA and Executive MBA/Small Business Programs.

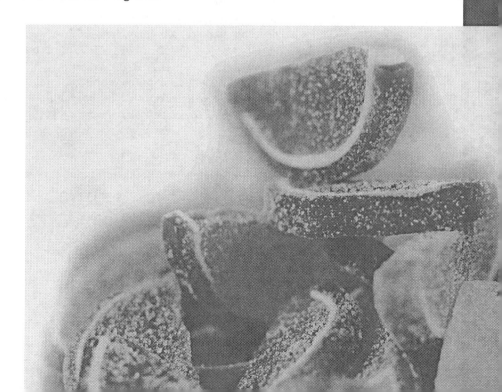

Taste Tested (or "Show-Me")

We know there is always a concern about new editions, but you might have noted that two of us teach in Missouri—the "show-me" state. Having a need to "show ourselves" that the book works, we class-tested it at the University of Missouri-Columbia for eight semesters prior to the first edition. We continue to use the book in our elementary course sequence. We used student and instructor feedback (from our institutions and others) to make the book even better. Here is what we found, and it has been confirmed by other class testers:

- Students liked reading this book.
- The writing style is "user friendly" so that the topics are very understandable.
- The end-of-chapter homework ties in well with the topical coverage in the chapters.
- The Solutions Manual is very clean.
- Instructors found the book to be clear and easy to teach from.

Furthermore, to assure ourselves that the homework and solutions were error-free, we wrote and checked all the homework items and solutions ourselves. In addition, all the solutions were accuracy-checked by graduate students and teaching assistants.

User Feedback

We would love to list all the positive quotes here that we've received from students and instructors who have used the book, but our editors say that would add significantly to the page count and thus to the cost of the book (which our marketing manager advises would result in negative comments from the students). So, we've listed one of each. This should help prove our point as well as illustrate that we have listened to the input of others in all stages of the development of this text.

"[Early in the first semester] I've had three students already tell me that they are really enjoying reading the text!! Wanted to let you know that I've been teaching accounting for 11 years and this is the first time I've ever heard any students make that comment. You should be very proud."
— Instructor, Winthrop University

"I enjoyed studying out of the book because it was written in a manner that is clear and easy to understand. The fact that the examples (Sweet Temptations, Unlimited Decadence) were used throughout the text was very helpful."

— Nathan Troup, Student

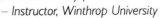

Kudos!

THIS BOOK IS A WORK IN PROCESS, AND WE WILL APPRECIATE YOUR FEEDBACK AND SUGGESTIONS FOR IMPROVEMENT AS IT EVOLVES INTO THE THIRD EDITION. BUT IT WOULDN'T HAVE PROGRESSED THIS FAR WITHOUT THE HELP, CREATIVE IDEAS, ENCOURAGEMENT, AND HARD WORK OF NUMEROUS INDIVIDUALS, INCLUDING THE FOLLOWING:

Reviewers

Elizabeth Ammann, Lindenwood University
Janice Benson, University of Wyoming
Kathy Brockway, Kansas State University at Salina
Steven Campbell, University of Idaho
David Collins, Bellarmine University
Lola Dudley, Eastern Illinois University
Jean Hartman, University of St. Thomas
Jerry Kreuze, Western Michigan University
Leonard Long, Bay State College
Tracy Manly, University of Tulsa

Ken Mark, Kansas City Community College
Melanie Middlemist, Colorado State University
Gary Olsen, Carroll College
Keith Patterson, Brigham Young University, Idaho
Franklin Plewa, Idaho State University
James Pofahl, University of Wisconsin, Oshkosh
Alexander Sannella, Rutgers Business School
Cinday Seipel, New Mexico State University
Fred Smith, Kansas State University
John Waters, II, University of Wyoming

Teaching Assistants/Class Testers at the University of Missouri-Columbia

Jaime Bierk
Marcia Bunten
David Chen
Cassi Costner
Rachel Davis
Carrie Duff
Gwen Ernst
John Faries
Katrinka Goldberg
Stacy Gower
Dave Gusky
Mark Gutwein
Mike Hart
Melissa Kahmann

Tim Koski
Lee Kraft
Shannon Lee
Jennifer Liesmann
Aaron Meinert
Holly Monks
Shannon Mudd
Lynn Nelson
Margaret Ofodile
Susan Parker
Cindy Patterson
Matt Peters
Katrina Pon
Mike Richey

Andrea Romi
Robbie Schoonmaker
Jennifer Seeser
Ken Smith
Dessie Stafford
Tom Stauder
Diane Sturek
Aaron Thorne
Robyn Vogt
Kelly Ward
Michael Weiss
Lisa Wright

Others who made invaluable contributions along the way:

Robin Roberts, University of Central Florida, and **James Stallman,** University of Missouri-Columbia, for significant contributions to earlier versions of several chapters in this book.

Tom Schmidt for his insightful (and inciteful) comments on critical and creative thinking.

Scott Summers and **Vairam Arunachalam,** and **Pat Wheeler,** University of Missouri-Columbia for their advice on certain database or computer issues.

Jennifer Seeser and **Diane Sturek** for the solutions they developed to the end-of-chapter homework.

David Chen, Cassi Costner, Herman Eckherle, Kelly Gallagher, Jason Janisse, Heather McWilliams, and **Emily Reinkemeyer** for their accuracy checks of these solutions.

Nathan (N8) Troup for his assistance in the development of certain aspects of the text and ancillaries.

Dana Cunningham for her Chapter 7 photograph.

Ed Scavone for his Chapter 7 quote.

Anita Blanchar for her meticulous typing of various ancillaries.

Karen Staggs for typing parts of the manuscript.

The thousands of students who endured the class testing of previous editions, especially those students who noticed and reported errors, inconsistencies, and typos in previous versions.

Those who made conscientious efforts toward the production of this book:

Glen Garrett our developmental editor, **Brian Schaefer** our production editor, **Cara Herman** our prepress specialist, and the compositor, **OffCenter Concept House**.

And thank you to all of the Cengage/South-Western and Cengage Learning Custom Solutions sales people for their observations, suggestions, and colossal past and future efforts to make this book known to those who dare to change.

Billie M. Cunningham
Loren A. Nikolai
John D. Bazley

ABOUT THE AUTHORS

Billie M. Cunningham

Billie Cunningham is an Associate Teaching Professor in the School of Accountancy at the University of Missouri-Columbia (MU). She has a wide variety of teaching experience, having taught graduate and/or undergraduate courses at private universities, public universities, and community colleges. She has received several awards for outstanding teaching, including a *2010 Teacher of the Year Award* from the Kansas City Robert J. Trulaske, Sr. College of Business Alumni chapter, a *2009 Grant-Thornton Teaching Excellence Award*, the *2008-2009 Robert J. Trulaske, Sr. College of Business Faculty Member of the Year*, a *2007 Williams-Keepers LLC Teaching Excellence Award in Accountancy*, the MU College of Business *2005-2006 Raymond F. and Mary A. O'Brien Excellence in Teaching Award*, an MU Student-Athlete Advisory Council *2004 Most Inspiring Professor Award*, *2000 Teacher of the Year Award*, from the Association of Accounting Students, *2000 Faculty Member of the Year Award* from the MU College of Business Student Council, *1998 Outstanding Faculty Award* from the Greek Councils of the University of Missouri-Columbia, and the *1995 Exemplary Accounting Educator Award* from the Missouri Association of Accounting Educators. Professor Cunningham has taught at Texas Christian University, University of Dallas, Collin County Community College, and the University of North Texas. She received her B.B.A., M.B.A. and Ph.D. from the University of North Texas. Professor Cunningham has conducted numerous workshops around the country on the use of writing exercises in accounting classes and on incorporating creative and critical thinking strategies into the accounting classroom. She was a coauthor of three previous textbooks.

Professor Cunningham has published articles in professional journals, including *Journal of Accounting Education, Issues in Accounting Education, Accounting Education: A Journal of Theory, Practice and Research, The CPA Journal, Research in Accounting Regulation, Management Accounting, Essays in Economic and Business History, The Community/Junior College Quarterly of Research and Practice Special Edition on College Teaching and Learning,* and *The Community/Junior College Quarterly of Research and Practice*. She received the *2010 Outstanding Research in Accounting Education Award* from the Teaching, Learning, and Curriculum Section of the American Accounting Association and the *1986–87 Outstanding Article Award* from the Two-Year College Section of the American Accounting Association. In addition, she serves on the Editorial Review Board of *Issues in Accounting Education*, the Editorial Advisory Board for *Accounting Education: An International Journal*, and has served as an ad hoc reviewer for *Advances in*

Accounting Education and *Journal of Accounting Education*. Professor Cunningham is the faculty advisor for Beta Alpha Psi at MU. As a member of the American Accounting Association (AAA), she served as Vice-President of the Association, as Chair of the Teaching, Learning, and Curriculum Section, and as Chair of the Two-Year College Section. She also has served on numerous AAA Committees. Professor Cunningham also has chaired, or served on, numerous Federation of Schools of Accountancy committees. She chaired the AICPA Core Competency Framework Best Practices Task Force and served on the AICPA Pre-certification Education Executive Committee. She currently serves as a Director of the Missouri Association of Accounting Educators. In fits of joy, Professor Cunningham sings in her car, dances in her living room, and teaches large-lecture classes (as well as normal-sized MBA classes).

Loren A. Nikolai

Loren Nikolai is the Ernst & Young Professor Emeritus in the School of Accountancy at the University of Missouri-Columbia (MU) where he has taught for over 30 years. He received his B.A. and M.B.A. from St. Cloud State University and his Ph.D. from the University of Minnesota. Professor Nikolai has taught at the University of Wisconsin at Platteville and at the University of North Carolina at Chapel Hill. Professor Nikolai has received an MU Student-Athlete Advisory Council *2004 Most Inspiring Professor Award*, the University of Missouri system-wide *1999 Presidential Award for Outstanding Teaching*, the MU College of Business and Public Administration *1999 Teacher of the Year Award*, the MU Alumni Association *1996 Faculty Award*, the MU College of Business and Public Administration *1994 Accounting Professor of the Year Award*, the Missouri Society of CPAs *1993 Outstanding Accounting Educator of the Year Award*, the MU *1992 Kemper Fellowship for Teaching Excellence*, the St. Cloud State University *1990 Distinguished Alumni Award*, and the Federation of Schools of Accountancy *1989 Faculty Award of Merit*, and was the co-recipient of the *1997 Holstein Creativity Award*. He holds a CPA certificate in the state of Missouri and previously worked for the 3M Company. Professor Nikolai is the lead author of *Intermediate Accounting*, Eleventh Edition (2010, South-Western Publishing Company). He was the lead author of two previous textbooks, *Principles of Accounting*, Third Edition (1990) and *Financial Accounting*, Third Edition (1990, PWS-Kent Publishing), and was the coauthor of *Financial Accounting: Concepts and Uses*, Third Edition (1995, South-Western Publishing).

Professor Nikolai has published numerous articles in *The Accounting Review, Journal of Accounting Research, The Accounting Educator's Journal, Journal of Accounting Education, The CPA Journal, Management Accounting, Policy Analysis, Academy of Management Journal, Journal of Business Research*, and other professional journals. He was also lead author of a monograph published by the National Association of Accountants. Professor Nikolai has served as an ad hoc reviewer for *The Accounting Review* and *Issues in Accounting Education*. He has made numerous presentations around the country on curricular and pedagogical issues in accounting education. Professor Nikolai was the Faculty Vice-President of the Beta Alpha Psi chapter at MU for 18 years. He is a member of the American Accounting Association, the American Institute of Certified Public Accountants (AICPA), and the Missouri Society of CPAs (MSCPA). He has served on the AICPA's Accounting and Auditing Practice Analysis Task Force Panel and the Accounting Careers Subcommittee; he has also served on the MSCPA's Relations with Educators, Accounting Careers, and Accounting and Auditing Committees. He is currently a member of the MSCPA Board of Directors and Educational Foundation. Professor Nikolai has chaired or served on numerous Federation of Schools of Accountancy (FSA) and American Accounting Association (AAA) committees, was AAA Director of Education for 1985–1987, and was President of the FSA for 1994. Professor Nikolai is married and has two adult children, three grandsons, and four stepchildren. His family has one cat, and he is an avid golfer and weight lifter.

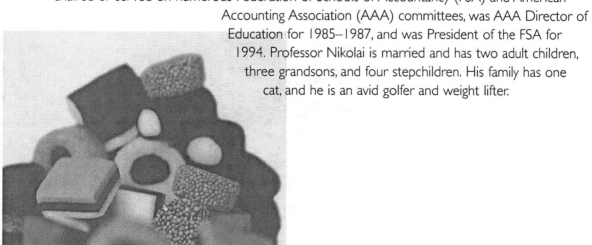

John D. Bazley

John D. Bazley, Ph.D., CPA, is the John J. Gilbert Professor of Accountancy in the School of Accountancy of the Daniels College of Business at the University of Denver where he has received *the University 1990 Distinguished Teaching Award, the Vernon Loomis Award for Excellence in Advising, the Alumni Award for Faculty Excellence, the Jerome Kesselman Endowment Award for Excellence in Research,* and the *1995 Cecil Puckett Award of the Daniels College of Business.* Professor Bazley earned a B.A. from the University of Bristol in England and an M.S. and Ph.D. from the University of Minnesota. He has taught at the University of North Carolina at Chapel Hill and holds a CPA certificate in Colorado. He has taught national professional development classes for a major CPA firm and was a consultant for another CPA firm. Professor Bazley is co-author of Intermediate Accounting, Eleventh Edition (2010, South-Western Publishing). He was also a co-author of *Principles of Accounting and Financial Accounting* (PWS-Kent Publishing Company).

Professor Bazley has published articles in professional journals including *The Accounting Review, Management Accounting, Accounting Horizons, Practical Accountant, Academy of Management Journal, The Journal of Managerial Issues,* and *The International Journal of Accounting,* and was a member of the Editorial Boards of *Issues in Accounting Education* and the *Journal of Managerial Issues.* He was also a co-author of a monograph on environmental accounting published by the National Association of Accountants. He has served as an expert witness for the Securities and Exchange Commission. He has served on numerous committees of The Federation of Schools of Accountancy (including Chair of the Student Lyceum Committee), the American Accounting Association, and the Colorado Society of CPAs (including the Continuing Professional Education Board and the Educational Foundation).

CHAPTER 1
**INTRODUCTION
TO BUSINESS,
ACCOUNTING,
AND DECISION
MAKING**

This section consists of one chapter which introduces you to business and accounting, and discusses the role of creative and critical thinking in business decisions. After reading this chapter, you will be able to:

- *understand the role of accounting information in business*

- *describe the planning, operating, and evaluating activities of managing a company*

- *know the difference between management accounting and finanacial accounting*

- *identify internal and external accounting reports*

- *explain the meaning of creative and critical thinking*

- *explain the role of creative and critical thinking in business decisions*

INTRODUCTION TO BUSINESS, ACCOUNTING, AND DECISION MAKING

"BUSINESS IS
A GAME, THE
GREATEST GAME
IN THE WORLD IF
YOU KNOW HOW TO
PLAY IT."

—THOMAS J.
WATSON SR.

1 Why is it necessary to have an understanding of business before trying to learn about accounting?

2 What is the role of accounting information within the business environment?

3 What is private enterprise, and what forms does it take?

4 What types of regulations do companies face?

5 What activities contribute to the operations of a company?

6 Are there any guidelines for reporting to company managers?

7 Are there any guidelines in the United States for reporting to people outside of a company?

8 What role does ethics play in the business environment?

9 What are creative and critical thinking?

10 What are the logical stages in problem solving and decision making?

What are you planning to do when you graduate from college—maybe become an accountant or a veterinarian, work your way up to marketing manager for a multinational company, manage the local food bank, or open a sporting goods store? Regardless of your career choice, you will be making business decisions, both in your personal life and at work. We have oriented this book to students like you who are interested in business and the role of accounting in business. You will see that accounting information, used properly, is a powerful tool for making good business decisions. People inside a business use accounting information to help determine and manage costs, set selling prices, and control the operations of the business. People outside the business use accounting information to help make investment and credit decisions about the business. Just what kinds of businesses use accounting? All of them! So let's take a little time to look at what *business* means.

Business affects almost every aspect of our lives. Think for a moment about your normal daily activities. How many businesses do you usually encounter? How many did you directly encounter today? Say you started the day with a quick trip to the local convenience store for milk and eggs. While you were out, you noticed that your car was low on fuel, so you stopped at the corner gas station. On the way to class, you dropped some clothes off at the cleaners. After your first class, you skipped lunch so that you could go to the bookstore and buy the calculator you need; after buying a candy bar for sustenance, you headed to your next class. In just half a day, you already interacted with four businesses: the convenience store, the gas station, the cleaners, and the bookstore.

 Actually, you encountered a fifth business, your school. Why would you describe your school as a business?

Although you were directly involved with four businesses, you were probably *affected* by hundreds of them. For example, two different businesses manufactured the calculator and the candy bar you purchased at the bookstore. Suppose that Unlimited Decadence Corporation manufactured the candy bar that you purchased. As we show in Exhibit 1-1, Unlimited Decadence purchased the candy bar ingredients from many other businesses *(suppliers)*. Each supplier provided Unlimited Decadence with particular ingredients. Shipping businesses *(carriers)* moved the ingredients from the suppliers' warehouses to Unlimited Decadence's factory. Then, after the candy bars were manufactured, a different carrier moved them from Unlimited Decadence to the bookstore. Making and shipping the calculator would follow the same process. You can see that many businesses are involved with manufacturing, shipping, and selling just two products. Now think about all the other products that you used during the morning and all the businesses that were involved with the manufacture and delivery of each product. Before leaving your house, apartment, or dorm this morning, you could easily have been affected by hundreds of businesses.

Products and services affect almost every minute of our lives, and businesses provide these products and services to us. As you will soon see, accounting plays a vital role in both businesses and the business environment by keeping track of a business's economic resources and economic activities, and then by reporting the business's financial position and the results of its activities to people who are interested in how well it is doing. (This is similar to the way statistics are gathered and reported for baseball players and other athletes.)

Accounting focuses on the resources and activities of individual businesses. We will introduce you to accounting by first looking at private enterprise and the environment in which businesses operate. Our discussion will include the types and forms of business, as well as some of the regulatory issues associated with forming and operating a business. Then we will discuss the activities of managers within a business. Next we will introduce the role of accounting information within a business and in the business environment. Finally, we will discuss the importance of ethics in business and accounting.

1 Why is it necessary to have an understanding of business before trying to learn about accounting?

2 What is the role of accounting information within the business environment?

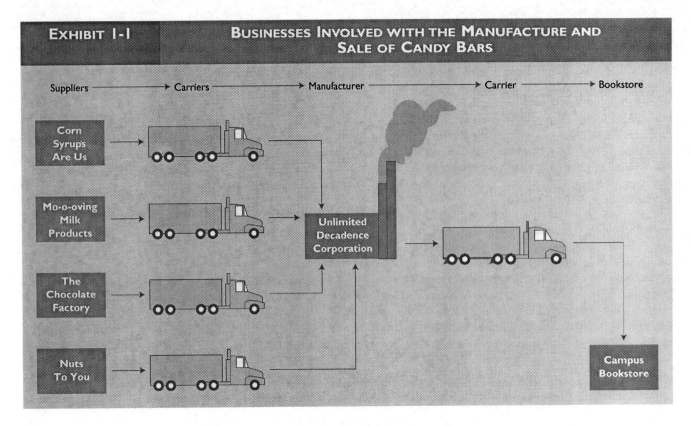

EXHIBIT 1-1   **BUSINESSES INVOLVED WITH THE MANUFACTURE AND SALE OF CANDY BARS**

PRIVATE ENTERPRISE AND CAPITALISM

3 What is private enterprise, and what forms does it take?

Businesses in the United States and most other countries operate in an economic system based on *private enterprise*. In this system, individuals (people like us, rather than public institutions like the government) own *companies* (businesses) that produce and sell services and/or goods for a profit. These companies generally fall into three categories: service companies, merchandising companies, and manufacturing companies.

Service Companies

Service companies perform services or activities that benefit individuals or business customers. The dry cleaning establishment where you dropped off your clothes this morning provides the service of cleaning and pressing your clothes for you. Companies like **Great Cuts**, **Midas**, **Merry Maids**, and **UPS**, and professional practices such as accounting, law, architecture, and medicine, are all service companies. Other companies in the private enterprise system produce or provide goods, or tangible, physical products. These companies can be either *merchandising companies* or *manufacturing companies*.

Merchandising Companies

Merchandising companies purchase goods (sometimes referred to as *merchandise* or *products*) for resale to their customers. Some merchandising companies, such as plumbing supply stores, electrical suppliers, or beverage distributors, are *wholesalers*. Wholesalers primarily sell their goods to retailers or other commercial users, like plumbers or electricians. Some merchandising companies, such as the bookstore where you bought your calculator and candy bar or the convenience store where you bought your milk and eggs, are *retailers*. Retailers sell their goods directly to the final customer or consumer. **JCPenney**, **Toys 'R' Us**, **amazon.com**, and **Best Buy** are retailers. Other examples of retailers include shoe stores and grocery stores.

Manufacturing Companies

Manufacturing companies make their products and then sell these products to their customers. Therefore, a basic difference between merchandising companies and manufacturing companies involves the products that they sell. Merchandising companies *buy* products that are physically ready for sale and then sell these products to their customers, whereas manufacturing companies *make* their products first and then sell the products to their customers. For example, the bookstore is a merchandising company that sells the candy bars it purchased from Unlimited Decadence, a manufacturing company. Unlimited Decadence, though, purchases (from suppliers) the chocolate, corn syrup, dairy products, and other ingredients to make the candy bars, which it then sells to the Campus Bookstore and other retail stores. **Apple Inc.**, **Stanley Black & Decker**, and **Dana Corporation** are examples of manufacturing companies. Exhibit 1-2 shows the relationship between manufacturing companies and merchandising companies and how they relate to their customers.

The line of distinction between service, merchandising, and manufacturing companies is sometimes blurry because a business can be more than one type of company. For example, Dell Computer Corporation manufactures personal computers, sells the computers it manufactures directly to business customers, government agencies, educational institutions, and individuals, and services those computers (through installation, technology transition, and management).

 Do you think a supplier to a manufacturing company is a merchandising company or a manufacturing company? Why?

Whether a company is a service, merchandising, or manufacturing company (or all three), for it to succeed in a private enterprise system, it must be able to obtain cash to begin to operate and then to grow. As we will discuss in the next sections, companies have several sources of cash.

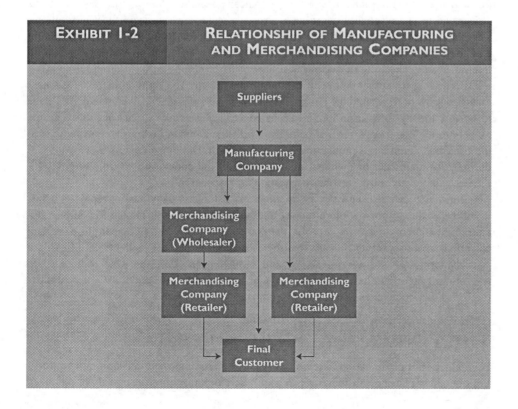

| EXHIBIT 1-2 | RELATIONSHIP OF MANUFACTURING AND MERCHANDISING COMPANIES |

Entrepreneurship and Sources of Capital

Owning a company involves a level of risk, along with a continuing need for **capital**. Although *capital* has several meanings, we use the term here to mean the funds a company needs to operate or to expand operations. In the next two sections we will discuss the risk involved with owning a company and possible sources of capital.

Entrepreneurship

Companies in a private enterprise system produce and sell services and goods for a profit. So, profit is the primary objective of a company. Profit rewards the company's owner or owners for having a business idea and for following through with that idea by investing time, talent, and money in the company. The company's owner hires employees, purchases land and a building (or signs a lease for space in a building), and purchases (or leases) any tools, equipment, machinery, and furniture necessary to produce or sell services or goods, *expecting, but not knowing for sure, that customers will buy what the company provides.* An individual who is willing to risk this uncertainty in exchange for the reward of earning a profit (and the personal reward of seeing the company succeed) is called an **entrepreneur**. Entrepreneurship, then, is a combination of three factors: the company owner's idea, the willingness of the company's owner to take a risk, and the abilities of the company's owner and employees to use capital to produce and sell goods or services. But where does the company get its capital?

Sources of Capital

One source of capital for a company is the entrepreneur's (or company owner's) investment in the company. An entrepreneur invests money "up front" so that the company can get started. The company uses the money to acquire the resources it needs to function. Then, as the company operates, the resources, or capital, of the company increase or decrease through the profits and losses of the company.

When an entrepreneur invests money in a company, he or she hopes to eventually get back the money he or she contributed to the company (a return *of* the contribution). Furthermore, the entrepreneur hopes to periodically receive additional money above the amount he or she originally contributed to the company (a return *on* the contribution). The entrepreneur would like the return *on* the contribution to be higher than the return that could have been earned with that same money on a different investment (such as an interest-bearing checking or savings account).

Borrowing is another source of capital for a company. To acquire the resources necessary to grow or to expand the types of products or services it sells, a company may have to borrow money from institutions like banks (called *creditors*). This occurs when the cash from the company's profits, combined with the company owner's contributions to the company, is not large enough to finance its growth. But borrowing by a company can be risky for the owner or owners. In some cases, if the company is unable to pay back the debt, the owner must personally assume that responsibility.

Borrowing can also be risky for a company. If the company cannot repay its debts, it will be unable to borrow more money and will soon find itself unable to continue operating. In addition to earning a profit, then, another objective of a company is to remain solvent. Remaining **solvent** means that the company can pay off its debts.

The terms *service, merchandising,* and *manufacturing* describe what companies do (perform services, purchase and sell goods, or make and sell products). We next discuss the forms that companies take, or how companies are organized.

THE FORMS THAT COMPANIES TAKE

Several types of organizations use accounting information in their decision-making functions but do not have profit-making as a goal. These organizations are called *not-for-profit*

EXHIBIT 1-3   **TYPES OF BUSINESS ORGANIZATIONS (COMPANIES)**

Sole Proprietorships
- Single owner-manager
- Small companies
- Most common type of business organization

Partnerships
- Two or more owners (partners)
- Partnership agreement

Corporations
- Stockholders have separate identity from company
- Capital stock
- Greatest volume of business

organizations and include many educational institutions, religious institutions, charitable organizations, municipalities, governments, and some hospitals. Since making a profit is not a goal of these organizations, some aspects of accounting for these organizations' activities are unique and beyond the scope of this book.

In this book we emphasize *business* organizations. These business organizations, or *companies,* are a significant aspect of the U.S. and world economies. As Exhibit 1-3 shows, a company may be organized as one of the following general types of business organizations: (1) sole proprietorship, (2) partnership, or (3) corporation.

Sole Proprietorships

A **sole proprietorship** is a company owned by one individual who is the sole investor of capital into the company. Usually the sole owner also acts as the manager of the company. Small retail stores and service firms often follow this form of organization. The sole proprietorship is the most common type of company because it is the easiest to organize and simplest to operate. In 2006, about 72 percent of all companies were sole proprietorships.[a]

Partnerships

A **partnership** is a company owned by two or more individuals (sometimes hundreds of individuals) who each invest capital, time, and/or talent into the company and share in the profits and losses of the company. These individuals are called *partners*, and their responsibilities, obligations, and benefits are usually described in a contract called a **partnership agreement**. Accounting firms and law firms are examples of partnerships. In 2006, just under 9 percent of all companies were partnerships.[b]

 If you and a friend decide to become business partners, do you think you need a formal partnership agreement? Why or why not?

Corporations

A **corporation** is a company organized as a separate legal entity, or body (separate from its owners), according to the laws of a particular state. In fact, the word *corporation* comes from the Latin word for body *(corpus).* In 2006, nearly 19 percent of all companies were corporations.[c]

By being incorporated, a company can enter into contracts, own property, and issue stock. A company issues shares of *capital stock* to owners, called *stockholders,* as evidence of the owners' investment of capital into the corporation. These shares are transferable from stockholder to stockholder, and each share represents part-ownership of the corporation. A corporation may be owned by one stockholder or by many stockholders (these stockholders are called *investors*). In fact, many large corporations have thousands of stockholders. For example, in their 2009 annual reports, **The Gap, Inc.** and **Intel Corporation** indicated that their stockholders owned 694 million and 5,562 million shares of stock, respectively!

The organization and legal structure of a corporation are more complex than that of a sole proprietorship or a partnership. Although sole proprietorships are the most common type of company, corporations conduct the greatest volume of business in the United States. In 2006, sole proprietorships made almost 5 percent, partnerships close to 12 percent, and corporations nearly 83 percent of all business sales in the United States.[d]

Since most of what we discuss in this text applies to all types of companies, we will use the general term *company* to apply to any company, regardless of structure. If the topic relates only to a specific type of company, we will identify the type of company.

THE REGULATORY ENVIRONMENT OF BUSINESS

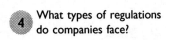
4 What types of regulations do companies face?

Companies affect each of us every day, but they also affect each other, the economy, and the environment. Just as individuals must abide by the laws and regulations of the cities, states, and countries in which they live and work, all companies, regardless of type, size, or complexity, must deal with regulatory issues.

Think again about that candy bar you had as a snack today. When Unlimited Decadence Corporation was formed, the company had to do more than build a factory, purchase equipment and ingredients, hire employees, find retail outlets to sell the candy bar, and begin operations. It also had to deal with the regulatory issues involved with opening and operating even the smallest of companies. Furthermore, its managers must continue to address regulatory issues as long as they continue to operate the company.

 Suppose a company is about to open a factory down the street from your house. What concerns do you have? What regulations might help reduce your concerns?

Many different laws and authorities regulate the business environment, covering issues such as consumer protection, environmental protection, employee safety, hiring practices, and taxes. Companies must comply with different sets of regulations depending on where their factories and offices are located. We discuss these sets of regulations next.

Local Regulations

City regulations involve matters such as zoning (parts of the city in which companies may operate), certificates of occupancy, and for some companies, occupational licenses and pollution control. Counties are concerned with issues such as the following: health permits for companies that handle, process, package, and warehouse food; registration of the unique name of each company; and control of pollution to air, land, or water.

State Regulations

States also regulate the activities of companies located within their borders. Most states require corporations to pay some form of state tax, usually an income tax (a tax on profit), a franchise tax (a fee for the privilege of conducting corporate business in the state), or both. New companies (regardless of form) in most states must apply for sales tax numbers and permits. Each state has unemployment taxes that companies operating within that state must pay.

Practicing professionals, such as doctors, lawyers, and accountants, must get a license for each state in which they practice. Finally, states regulate companies that conduct certain types of business. For example, in Texas, companies that sell, transport, or store alcoholic beverages must obtain licenses from, and pay fees to, the state of Texas. Massachusetts regulations ban selling fireworks, whereas New Hampshire allows the sale of fireworks.

Federal Regulations

The federal government has a variety of laws and agencies that regulate companies and the business environment. These laws and agencies relate to specific aspects and activities of companies, regardless of the city or state in which the companies are located.

Internal Revenue Service

All companies have some dealings with the Internal Revenue Service (IRS). Each company must withhold taxes from its employees' pay and send these taxes to the IRS. Furthermore, the IRS taxes the profits of the companies themselves. The type of company determines who actually pays the taxes on profits, though. Corporations must pay their own income taxes to the IRS because, from a legal standpoint, they are viewed as being separate from their owners. Sole proprietorships and partnerships, however, do not pay taxes on their profits. Rather, owners of these types of companies include their share of the company profits along with their other taxable income on their personal income tax returns. This is because the tax law does not distinguish the owners of sole proprietorships and partnerships from the companies themselves.

Laws and Other Government Agencies

A variety of laws and government departments and agencies (in addition to the IRS) regulate companies. Federal departments and agencies oversee the administration of laws governing areas such as competition (the Federal Trade Commission and the Department of Justice), fair labor practices (the Department of Labor), safety (the Occupational Safety and Health Administration), employee and customer accessibility (the Department of Justice), workplace discrimination (the Equal Employment Opportunity Commission), control of pollution to air, land, or water (the Environmental Protection Agency), and the like.

International Regulations

When a company conducts business internationally, it also must abide by the laws and regulations of the other countries in which it operates. These laws and regulations address such issues as foreign licensing, export and import documentation requirements, tax laws, multinational production and marketing regulations, domestic ownership of company property, and expatriation of cash (how much of the company's cash can leave the country). Of course, these laws and regulations differ from country to country, so a company operating in several countries must abide by many laws and regulations. Exhibit 1-4

EXHIBIT 1-4	COMMON REGULATORY ISSUES COMPANIES FACE		
City and County Issues	**State Issues**	**Federal Issues**	**International Issues**
zoning	state tax	federal taxes	foreign licensing
certificate of occupancy	sales tax	competition	exports and imports
occupational license	unemployment taxes	labor standards	taxes
environmental regulations	professional licenses	working conditions	multinational production and
health permit	industry-specific regulations	workplace discrimination	marketing
company name and registration			property ownership
			cash restrictions

lists some of the more common regulatory issues facing companies operating in different jurisdictions.

 Suppose that as a manager of a manufacturing company, you have the opportunity to have many parts of your product manufactured in another country where the labor is much cheaper and the environmental regulations are less stringent. What are the pros and cons of taking advantage of this opportunity?

INTEGRATED ACCOUNTING SYSTEM

A company is responsible to many diverse groups of people, both inside and outside the company. For example, its managers and employees depend on the company for their livelihood. Customers expect a dependable product or service at a reasonable cost. The community expects the company to be a good citizen. Owners want returns on their investments, and creditors expect to be paid back. Governmental agencies expect companies to abide by their rules.

People in all of these groups use accounting information about the company to help them assess a company's ability to carry out its responsibilities, and to help them make decisions involving the company. This information comes from the company's integrated accounting system. An **integrated accounting system** is a means by which accounting information about a company's activities is identified, measured, recorded, and summarized so that it can be communicated in an accounting report. A company's integrated accounting system provides much of the information used by the many diverse groups of people outside the company (these are sometimes called **external users**), as well as by the managers and employees within the company (these are sometimes called **internal users**). Two branches of accounting, management accounting and financial accounting, use the information in the integrated accounting system to produce reports for different groups of people. Management accounting provides vital information about a company to internal users; financial accounting gives information about a company to external users.

Management Accounting Information

Management accounting information helps managers plan, operate, and evaluate a company's activities. Managers must operate the company in a changing environment. They need information to help them compete in a world market in which technology and methods of production are constantly changing. Moreover, in a world exploding with new information, managers must manage that information in a way that will let them use it more efficiently and effectively. Accounting is one of the critical tools of information management.

Since management accounting helps managers inside the company, it is free from the restrictions of regulatory bodies interested in how companies report to external users. Therefore, managers can request "tailor made" information in whatever form is useful for their decision making, such as in dollars, units, hours worked, products manufactured, numbers of defective units, or service agreements signed. The integrated accounting system provides information about segments of the company, products, tasks, plants, or individual activities, depending on what information is important for the decisions managers are making.

Financial Accounting Information

Financial accounting information is organized for the use of interested people outside of the company. External users analyze the company's financial reports as one source of useful financial information about the company. For these users to be able to interpret the reports, companies reporting to outsiders follow specific guidelines, or rules, known as *generally accepted accounting principles,* (almost a one-size-fits-all approach to reporting). Since a company's financial reports are not tailored to specific user decisions, external users have to use care to find the information in these reports that is relevant to their decisions.

Financial accounting information developed by the integrated accounting system is expressed in dollars in the United States and in different currencies (such as yen, euros, and pesos) in other countries. This information emphasizes the whole company and sometimes important segments of the company.

Both internal and external users need accounting information to make decisions about a company. Since external users want to see the reported results of management activities, we discuss these activities next. Then we will discuss how accounting information supports both management activities and external decision making.

MANAGEMENT ACTIVITIES

Managers play a vital role in a company's success—by setting goals, making decisions, committing the resources of the company to achieving these goals, and then by achieving these goals. To help ensure the achievement of these goals and the success of the company, managers use accounting information as they perform the activities of planning the operations of the company, operating the company, and evaluating the operations of the company for future planning and operating decisions. Exhibit 1-5 shows these activities.

⑤ What activities contribute to the operations of a company?

Planning

Management begins with planning. A clear plan lays out the organization of, and gives direction to, the operating and evaluating activities. **Planning** establishes the company's goals and the means of achieving these goals. Managers use the planning process to identify what resources and employees the company needs in order to achieve its goals. They also use the planning process to set standards, or "benchmarks," against which they later can measure the company's progress toward its goals. Periodically measuring the company's progress against standards or benchmarks helps managers identify whether the company needs to make corrections to keep itself on course. Because the business environment changes so rapidly, plans must be ongoing and flexible enough to deal with change before it occurs or as it is happening.

Managers of companies operating in more than one country have more to consider in their planning process than do those operating only in the United States. Managers of multinational companies must also consider such factors as multiple languages, economic systems, political systems, monetary systems, markets, and legal systems. In such companies, managers must also plan and encourage the communication between and among branches in several countries.

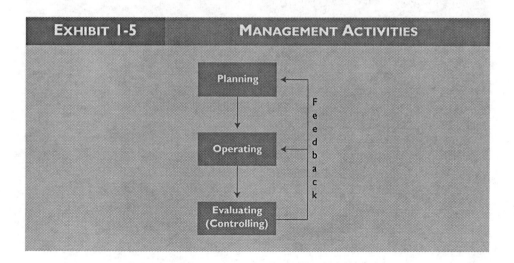

| EXHIBIT 1-5 | MANAGEMENT ACTIVITIES |

Operating

Operating refers to the set of activities that the company engages in to conduct its business according to its plan. For Unlimited Decadence, these are the activities that ensure that candy bars get made and sold. They involve gathering the resources and employees necessary to achieve the goals of the company, establishing organizational relationships among departments and employees, and working toward achieving the goals of the company. In operating the company, managers and work teams must make day-to-day decisions about how best to achieve these goals. For example, accounting information gives them valuable data about a product's performance. With this information, they can decide which products to continue to sell and when to add new products or drop old ones. If the company is a manufacturing company, managers and work teams can decide what products to produce and whether there is a better way to produce them. With accounting information, managers can also make decisions about how to set product selling prices, whether to advertise and how much to spend on advertising, and whether to buy new equipment or expand facilities. These decisions are ongoing and depend on managers' evaluations of the progress being made toward the company's goals and on changes in the company's plans and goals.

Evaluating

Evaluating is the management activity that measures actual operations and progress against standards or benchmarks. It provides feedback for managers to use to correct deviations from those standards or benchmarks, and to plan for the company's future operations. Evaluating is a continuous process that attempts to prevent problems or to detect and correct problems as quickly as possible.

As you might guess, the more countries in which a company operates, the more interesting the evaluating activity becomes. Because of cultural and other differences, evaluation methods and feedback used in some countries may have little meaning in other countries. For example, it would be difficult to convince employees of the importance of high quality if these employees are used to standing in long lines for whatever quality and quantity of merchandise is available in their country. Managers must pay particular attention to the cultural effects of evaluation methods and feedback in order to achieve effective control.

Do you think these people are engaged in planning activities, operating activities, or evaluating activities? Why?

© RYAN McVAY/GETTY IMAGES

Even coaches of professional sports teams perform the activities of planning, operating, and evaluating. If a team's goal is to win the Super Bowl, how would the head coach implement each of these activities?

Planning, operating, and evaluating all require information about the company. The company's accounting system provides much of the quantitative information managers use.

ACCOUNTING SUPPORT FOR MANAGEMENT ACTIVITIES

Management accounting involves identifying, measuring, recording, summarizing, and then communicating economic information about a company to *internal* users for management decision-making. Internal users include individual employees, work groups or teams, departmental supervisors, divisional and regional managers, and "top management." Management accountants, then, provide information to internal users for planning the operations of the company, for operating the company, and for evaluating the operations of the company. With the help of the management accountant, managers use this information to help them make decisions about the company.

The reports that result from management accounting can help managers *plan* the activities and resources needed to achieve the goals of the company. These reports may provide revenue (amounts charged to customers) estimates and cost estimates of planned activities and resources, and an analysis of these cost estimates. By describing how alternative actions might affect the company's profit and solvency, these estimates and analyses help managers plan.

In *operating* a company, managers use accounting information to make day-to-day decisions about what activities will best achieve the goals of the company. Management accounting helps managers make these decisions by providing timely economic information about how each activity might affect profit and solvency.

Accounting information also plays a vital role in helping managers *evaluate* the operations of the company. Managers use the revenue and cost estimates generated during the planning and decision-making process as a benchmark, and then compare the company's actual revenues and costs against that benchmark to evaluate how well the company is carrying out its plans.

Since managers are making decisions about their own company, and since each company is different, the information the management accountant provides must be "custom fitted" to the information needs of the company. This involves selecting the appropriate information to report, presenting that information in an understandable format (interpreting the information when necessary), and providing the information when it is needed for the decisions being made.

Management accounting responsibilities and activities thus vary widely from company to company. Furthermore, these responsibilities and activities continue to evolve as management accountants respond to the need for new information—a need caused by the changing business environment.

In response to this changing business environment, the Institute of Management Accountants (IMA) publishes guidelines for management accountants called Statements on Management Accounting (SMAs).

Statements on Management Accounting

SMAs serve as guidelines for management accountants to use in fulfilling their responsibilities. The SMAs are nonbinding (they are not rules that must be followed), but because they are developed by professional accountants, as well as leaders in industry and colleges and universities, management accountants turn to SMAs for help when faced with new situations.

6 Are there any guidelines for reporting to company managers?

Framework for Management Accounting

The responsibility for identifying issues to be addressed by SMAs lies with an IMA committee called the Management Accounting Practices Committee. One of the first activities this committee undertook was to develop a framework for the work it was assigned to do. The framework developed by this committee defines the scope of the SMAs, including a statement of the objectives of management accounting and a description of the activities and responsibilities of management accountants.[e]

Company-specific responsibilities and unique elements of a company's internal reports may change, but the underlying goals of management accounting remain the same for all companies:

- To inform people inside and outside the company about past or future events or circumstances that affect the company
- To interpret information from inside and outside the company and to communicate the implications of this information to various segments of the company
- To establish planning and control systems that ensure that company employees use the company's resources in accordance with company policy
- To develop information systems (manual or computer systems) that contain, process, and manage accounting data
- To implement the use of modern equipment and techniques to aid in identifying, gathering, analyzing, communicating, and protecting information
- To ensure that the accounting system provides accurate and reliable information
- To develop and maintain an effective and efficient management accounting organization

To see how a company's accounting information helps managers in their planning, operating, and evaluating activities, briefly consider three key management accounting reports prepared with these goals in mind.

Basic Management Accounting Reports

Budgets, cost analyses, and manufacturing cost reports are examples of management tools the accounting system provides. Exhibit 1-6 illustrates the relationships between management activities and these reports.

 Suppose you are the manager of your company's sales force. What type of information would you want to help you do your job?

Budgets
Budgeting is the process of quantifying managers' plans and showing the impact of these plans on the company's operating activities and financial position. Managers present this information in a report called a *budget* (or *forecast*). Once the planned activities have occurred, managers can evaluate the results of the operating activities against the budget to make sure that the actual operations of the various parts of the company achieved the established plans. For example, Unlimited Decadence might develop a budget showing how many boxes of candy bars it plans to sell during the first three months of 2011. Later, after actual 2011 sales have been made, managers will compare the results of these sales with the budget to determine if their forecasts were "on target" and, if not, to find out why differences occurred. We will discuss budgets further in Chapters 3 and 11.

Cost Analyses
Cost analysis, or **cost accounting**, is the process of determining and evaluating the costs of specific products or activities within a company. Managers use cost analyses when making decisions about these products or activities. For example, Unlimited Decadence

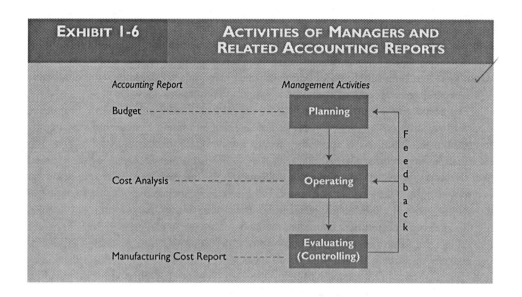

EXHIBIT 1-6   **ACTIVITIES OF MANAGERS AND RELATED ACCOUNTING REPORTS**

might use a cost analysis to decide whether to stop or to continue making the Divinely Decadent candy bar. The cost analysis report might show that the candy bar is not profitable because it earns less than it costs to make. If this is the case, the fact that this candy bar does not make a profit will be one factor in the managers' decision. The company's managers also will have to resolve the ethical issue of whether to lay off the employees who produced the candy bar. (Can you think of an alternative to a layoff?)

Suppose you are a manager of a company that makes a food product thought to create major health problems after long-term use. What facts would you consider in trying to decide whether the company should drop the product or continue producing it?

We will discuss cost analysis reports again in Chapter 14 in Volume 2.

Manufacturing Cost Reports

As we mentioned above, managers must monitor and evaluate a company's operations to determine if its plans are being achieved. Accounting information can highlight specific "variances" from plans, indicating where corrections to operations can be made if necessary.

For example, a manufacturing cost report might show that total actual costs for a given month were greater than total budgeted costs. However, it might also show that some actual costs were greater than budgeted costs while others were less than budgeted costs. The more detailed information will be useful for managers as they analyze why these differences occurred, and then make adjustments to the company's operations to help the company achieve its plans. We will discuss manufacturing cost reports again in Chapter 16 in Volume 2.

ACCOUNTING SUPPORT FOR EXTERNAL DECISION MAKING

Say you have been offered a job at Unlimited Decadence. What economic information concerning Unlimited Decadence would you want to know about to help you decide whether to accept the job offer?

Management accounting gives people inside a company vital business information about the company and its performance, but the company also must provide business information about its performance to people outside the company. **Financial accounting** involves identifying, measuring, recording, summarizing, and then communicating economic information about a company to *external* users for use in their various decisions. External users are people and groups outside the company who need accounting information to decide whether or not to engage in some activity with the company. These users include individual investors, stockbrokers and financial analysts who offer investment assistance, consultants, bankers, suppliers, labor unions, customers, and local, state, and federal governments and governments of countries in which the company does business.

The accounting information that helps external users make a decision (for example, a bank's loan officer deciding whether or not to extend a loan to a company) may be different from the information a manager within the company needs. Thus the accounting information prepared for the external user may differ from that prepared for the internal user. However, some of the accounting information the internal user needs also helps the external user and vice versa. For example, Unlimited Decadence may decide to continue to produce and sell a new candy bar if it can borrow enough money to do so. In weighing the likelihood of getting a loan from the bank, company managers will probably want to evaluate the same financial accounting information that the bank evaluates. In deciding whether to make a loan to Unlimited Decadence, the bank will consider the likelihood that Unlimited Decadence will repay the loan. Since this likelihood may depend on current and future sales of the candy bar, the bank also may want to evaluate the company's actual sales, as well as the sales budget that Unlimited Decadence's managers developed as part of the planning process.

Many external users evaluate the accounting information of more than one company, and need comparable information from each company. For example, a bank looks at accounting information from all of its customers who apply for loans, and must use comparable information in order to decide to which customers it will make loans. This need for comparability creates a need for guidelines or rules for companies to follow when preparing accounting information for external users. Over the years, because of the activities of several professional accounting organizations, a set of broad guidelines for financial accounting has evolved in the United States. These guidelines are referred to as *generally accepted accounting principles.*

Generally Accepted Accounting Principles

7 Are there any guidelines in the United States for reporting to people outside of a company?

Generally accepted accounting principles, or **GAAP**, are the currently accepted principles, procedures, and practices that companies use for financial accounting and reporting in the United States. These principles, or "rules," must be followed in the external reports of companies that sell capital stock to the public in the United States and by many other companies as well. GAAP covers such issues as how to account for inventory, buildings, income taxes, and capital stock; how to measure the results of a company's operations; and how to account for the operations of companies in specialized industries, such as the banking industry, the entertainment industry, and the insurance industry. Without these agreed-upon principles, external users of accounting information would not be able to understand the meaning of this information. (Imagine if we all tried to communicate with each other without any agreed-upon rules of spelling and grammar!)

Several organizations contribute to GAAP through their publications (called "pronouncements" or "standards"). The two most important organizations that develop GAAP in the United States are the Financial Accounting Standards Board (FASB) and the Securities and Exchange Commission (SEC). The FASB is a five-member full-time board of professional accountants and businesspeople. Its standards are included in the *FASB Accounting Standards Codification™* (or, simply, the Codification). The Codification is an electronic database located at http://asc.fasb.org. This Codification is the only source of U.S. GAAP for most companies.[1] The SEC is a branch of the U.S. government; it has the legal authority to prescribe accounting principles and reporting practices for all cor-

---

[1]An exception to this rule are publicly traded corporations which are also subject to GAAP set by the SEC, as we discuss later.

porations issuing publicly traded capital stock. The SEC issues *Financial Reporting Releases* containing financial accounting guidelines.

International Financial Reporting Standards

Accounting has been less standardized worldwide than in the United States because of cultural, legal, economic, and other differences among countries. However, with the increase in U.S. and foreign companies doing international business, international accounting rules are becoming more important. Several organizations have made progress in developing worldwide accounting standards. Most notably, the International Accounting Standards Board (IASB) has issued nearly 50 standards covering issues such as accounting for inventories, property and equipment, and the results of a company's operations. These standards are called **International Financial Reporting Standards,** or **IFRS.** The accounting and reporting "rules" established in many IFRS are very similar to GAAP, but there are some differences. In a move toward more standard reporting among companies conducting international business, the SEC has issued a proposal that starting in 2014, all corporations regulated by it (those issuing publicly traded capital stock) must begin using IFRS instead of GAAP. Generally, companies regulated by the SEC are very large corporations and these companies will be most affected by this ruling.

In Volume 1 of this book, we deal primarily with sole proprietorships, partnerships, or small corporations which generally are subject to GAAP rather than IFRS. For these companies, we will discuss GAAP rules that apply to their accounting issues. However, many GAAP pronouncements are complex and very technical in nature. Therefore, we will introduce only the basic aspects of GAAP. In Volume 2 of this book, we discuss accounting issues dealing with large corporations. We will continue to discuss GAAP because its rules apply to these companies, but where the rules under IFRS differ from GAAP, we also will briefly discuss these differences.

Basic Financial Statements

Companies operate to achieve various goals. They may be interested in providing a healthy work environment for their employees, in reaching a high level of pollution control, or in making contributions to civic and social organizations and activities. However, to meet these goals, a company must first achieve its two primary objectives: *earning a satisfactory profit* and *remaining solvent*. If a company fails to meet either of these objectives, it will not be able to achieve its various goals and will not be able to survive in the long run.

Profit (commonly referred to as *net income*) is the difference between the cash and credit sales of a company *(revenues)* and its total costs *(expenses)*. **Solvency** is a company's long-term ability to pay its debts as they come due. As you will see, both internal and external users analyze the *financial statements* of a company to determine how well the company is achieving its two primary objectives.

Financial statements are accounting reports used to summarize and communicate financial information about a company. A company's integrated accounting system produces three major financial statements: the income statement, the balance sheet, and the cash flow statement. It also produces a supporting financial statement: the statement of changes in owner's equity. Each of these statements summarizes specific information that has been identified, measured, and recorded during the accounting process.

Income Statement

A company's **income statement** summarizes the results of its operating activities for *a specific time period* and shows the company's profit for that period. It shows a company's revenues, expenses, and net income (or net loss) for that time period, usually one year. Exhibit 1-7 shows what kind of information appears in a company's income statement. **Revenues** are the prices charged to a company's customers for the goods or services the company provided to them. **Expenses** are the costs of providing the goods or services. These amounts include the costs of the products the company has sold (either the cost of making these products or the cost of purchasing these products), the costs of conducting

EXHIBIT 1-7	WHAT A COMPANY'S INCOME STATEMENT SHOWS

Revenues

Here's where the company shows what it charged customers for the goods or services provided to them during a specific time period.

Expenses

Here's where the company lists the costs of providing the goods and services during that period.

Net Income

This is the difference between revenues and expenses.

business (called *operating expenses*), and the costs of income taxes, if any. The **net income** is the excess of revenues over expenses, or the company's profit; a **net loss** arises when expenses are greater than revenues. We will discuss the income statement further in Chapter 6 and throughout the book.

Balance Sheet

A company's **balance sheet** summarizes its financial position *on a given date* (usually the last day of the time period covered by the income statement). It is also called a *statement of financial position*. Exhibit 1-8 shows what kind of information appears on a balance sheet. A balance sheet lists the company's assets, liabilities, and owner's equity on the given date. **Assets** are economic resources that a company owns and that it expects will provide future benefits to the company. **Liabilities** are the company's economic obligations (debts) to its creditors—people outside the company such as banks and suppliers—and to its employees. The **owner's equity** of a company is the owner's current investment in the assets of the company, which includes the owner's contributions to the company and any earnings (net income) that the owner leaves in (or invests in) the company. A corporation's owners' equity is called **stockholders' equity**. We will discuss the balance sheet further in Chapter 6 and throughout the book.

Statement of Changes in Owner's Equity

A company's integrated accounting system frequently provides a supporting financial statement, called a **statement of changes in owner's equity**, to explain the amount shown in the owner's equity section of the company's balance sheet. Both the balance sheet and the statement of changes in owner's equity show the owner's investment in the assets of the company on the balance sheet date. However, the statement of changes in owner's equity also summarizes the *changes* that occurred in the owner's investment between the first day and the last day of the time period covered by the company's income statement.

EXHIBIT 1-8	WHAT A COMPANY'S BALANCE SHEET SHOWS

Assets	**Liabilities**
Here's where the company lists its economic resources, such as cash, inventories of its products, and equipment it owns.	Here's where the company lists its obligations to creditors, such as banks and suppliers, and to employees.
	Owner's Equity
	Here's where the company lists the owner's current investment in the assets of the company.

EXHIBIT 1-9	WHAT A COMPANY'S STATEMENT OF CHANGES IN OWNER'S EQUITY SHOWS

Beginning Owner's Equity

Here's where the company shows the Owner's Equity amount at the beginning of the income statement period (the last day of the previous income statement period). This amount also appears on the balance sheet on the last day of the previous income statement period.

+ Net Income

Here's where the company adds the net income from the period's Income Statement (the profit that the company earned during the income statement period).

+ Owner's Contributions

Here's where the company adds any additional contributions to the company that the company's owner made during the income statement period.

– Withdrawals

Here's where the company subtracts any withdrawals of cash from the company that the company's owner made during the income statement period.

Ending Owner's Equity

Here's where the company shows the resulting Owner's Equity amount that also appears on the company's balance sheet on the last day of the income statement period.

Exhibit 1-9 shows the kind of changes in owner's equity that appear on this statement. Net income earned during the period increases the owner's investment in the company's assets (and the assets themselves) as the owner "reinvests" the profit of the company back into the company. Similarly, additional contributions of money by the owner to the company during the time period also increase the owner's investment in the company's assets (and the assets themselves). On the other hand, a net loss, rather than a net income, decreases the owner's investment in the company (and the company's assets), as does the owner's choice to remove (or withdraw) money from the company ("disinvesting" the profit from the company). We will discuss the statement of changes in owner's equity further in Chapter 5 and throughout the book.

Cash Flow Statement

A company's **cash flow statement** summarizes its cash receipts, cash payments, and net change in cash for a specific time period. Exhibit 1-10 shows what kind of information appears in a cash flow statement. The cash receipts and cash payments for operating activities, such as products sold or services performed and the costs of producing the products or services, are summarized in the *cash flows from operating activities* section of the statement. The cash receipts and cash payments for investing activities are summarized in the *cash flows from investing activities* section of the statement. Investing activities include the purchases and sales of assets such as buildings and equipment. The cash receipts and cash payments for financing activities, such as money borrowed from and repaid to banks, are summarized in the *cash flows from financing activities* section of the statement. We will discuss the cash flow statement further in Chapter 7, and throughout the book.

A company may publish its income statement, balance sheet, and cash flow statement (and statement of changes in owner's equity), along with other related financial accounting information, in its **annual report**. Many companies (mostly corporations) do so. We will discuss the content of an annual report in Chapter 9.

ETHICS IN BUSINESS AND ACCOUNTING

A company's financial statements are meant to convey information about the company to internal and external users in order to help them make decisions about the company. But if the

EXHIBIT 1-10	WHAT A COMPANY'S CASH FLOW STATEMENT SHOWS

Cash Flows from Operating Activities

Here's where the company lists the cash it received and paid in selling products or performing services for a specific time period.

Cash Flows from Investing Activities

Here's where the company lists the cash it received and paid in buying and selling assets such as equipment and buildings.

Cash Flows from Financing Activities

Here's where the company lists the cash it received and paid in obtaining and repaying bank loans and from contributions and withdrawals of cash made by the company's owners.

information in the financial statements does not convey a realistic picture of the results of the company's operations or its financial position, the decisions based on this information can have disastrous consequences.

Consider the fallout from Enron Corporation's 2001 financial statements.[f] On October 1, 2001, Enron Corporation was the seventh-largest company in the United States, employing 21,000 people in more than 40 countries. It was also the largest energy trading company in the United States. *Fortune* magazine had ranked Enron 24th in its "100 Best Companies to Work for in America" in the year 2000.[g] It's stock was trading for about $83 per share. Two weeks later, after reporting incredible profits for its first two quarters (January through June) of 2001, Enron reported a third-quarter (July through September) loss, in part because of adjustments caused by previously misstated profits. But by November 1, JP Morgan Chase and Citigroup's Salomon Smith Barney had attempted to rescue Enron by extending the company an opportunity to borrow $1 billion (above what Enron already owed them). On November 19, Enron publicly acknowledged that its financial statements did not comply with GAAP in at least two areas. This failure resulted in huge misstatements on Enron's financial statements: assets and profits were overstated, and liabilities were understated. On December 2, 2001, Enron declared bankruptcy.

The rapid demise of one of the largest, and what appeared to be one of the most successful, companies in the world to the largest corporate failure in the United States created a wave of economic and emotional effects around the world. Before Enron reported a third-quarter loss, its stock was selling for around $83 per share. After Enron reported its loss, its stock dropped to $0.70 per share—a total drop in market value of almost $60 billion. Most of those who had purchased shares of Enron stock lost money. Many lost hundreds of thousands of dollars! The Enron employees' pension plan, 62 percent of which was Enron stock, lost nearly $2.1 billion dollars, virtually wiping out the retirement savings of most of Enron's employees, many of whom were nearing retirement age. Close to 5,600 Enron employees were laid off from their jobs. Enron left approximately $63 billion in debts, with JP Morgan owed $900 million and Citigroup up to $800 million. Many banks around the world also were affected by having lent money to Enron.

In addition to these after-effects, the Justice Department prosecuted the accounting firm Arthur Andersen—Enron's auditor. It claimed that Anderson had interfered with the federal investigation of Enron's collapse by shredding paperwork related to Anderson's audit of Enron. Two Andersen executives—a partner and an in-house attorney—had reminded employees of Andersen's document destruction policy during the time that the Justice Department was investigating Enron's failure, resulting in large-scale shredding of the Enron documents. A jury found Andersen guilty. As a result, Arthur Andersen, a highly respected accounting firm and bastion of integrity, relinquished its accounting license, preventing it from conducting audits. Andersen, a once-thriving company of 28,000 em-

8 What role does ethics play in the business environment?

ployees shriveled to 200. Ironically, too late for the employees who had lost their jobs, the Supreme Court found that the jurors in this case had received improper instructions, and it rejected the Justice Department's claim, vindicating Arthur Andersen.[h]

Ethical behavior on the part of all of Enron's managers would not have guaranteed the company's success. However, it could have prevented much of the damage suffered by those inside and outside the company, including those who depended on Enron's financial statements to provide them with dependable information about the company.

Do you think JP Morgan or Citigroup would have lent Enron as much money if Enron had not overstated its net income and assets, and understated its liabilities? Why or why not? What might Enron's employees have done differently if Enron's financial statements had been properly stated?

Enron was not the first nor (unfortunately) the last company to get into trouble for misleading financial reporting. More recently in 2009 Bernard Madoff, the owner of successful money management firm Bernard L. Madoff Investment Securities LLC., was sentenced to *150 years* in prison for what might be the largest swindle in Wall Street history. Using a ponzi scheme (paying back early investments with the money of more recent investments), Madoff defrauded thousands of investors of about $65 billion. Many investors lost their life savings. Among the 11 felony charges to which he pled guilty were securities fraud, investment adviser fraud, false filings with the SEC, and theft from an employee benefit plan. While it seems clear that some of what Enron's managers, Bernard Madoff, and managers of some other companies disclosed on their financial statements was wrong, many business and accounting issues and events in the business environment cannot be interpreted as absolutely right or wrong. Every decision or choice has pros and cons, costs and benefits, and people or institutions who will be affected positively or negatively by the decision. Even in a setting where many issues and events fall between the extremes of right and wrong, it is very important for accountants and businesspeople to maintain high ethical standards. Several groups have established codes of ethics addressing ethical behavior to help accountants and their business associates work their way through the complicated ethical issues associated with business issues and events. These groups include the American Institute of Certified Public Accountants (AICPA), the Institute of Management Accountants (IMA), the International Federation of Accountants (IFAC), and most large companies.

Professional Organizations' Codes of Ethics

The members of the AICPA adopted a code of professional conduct that guides them in their professional work.[i] It addresses such issues as self-discipline, honorable behavior, moral judgments, the public interest, professionalism, integrity, and technical and ethical standards. The IMA has a code of conduct that is similar to the AICPA's code.[j] It addresses competence, confidentiality, integrity, credibility, and resolution of ethical conflict.

The IFAC is an independent, worldwide organization. Its stated purpose is to "develop and enhance a coordinated worldwide accountancy profession with harmonized standards." As part of its efforts, it has developed a code of ethics for accountants in each country to use as the basis for founding their own codes of ethics.[k] Because of the wide cultural, language, legal, and social diversity of the nations of the world, the IFAC expects professional accountants in each country to add their own national ethical standards to the code to reflect their national differences, or even to delete some items of the code at their national level. The code addresses objectivity, resolution of ethical conflicts, professional competence, confidentiality, tax practice, cross-border activities, and publicity. It also addresses independence, fees and commissions, activities incompatible with the practice of accountancy, clients' money, relations with other professional accountants, and advertising and solicitation.

Ethics at the Company Level

Even before the collapse of Enron, many companies developed codes or statements of company and business ethics. For example, **Texas Instruments Incorporated (TI)**, which manufactures microchips, calculators, and other electronic equipment, has several documents containing guidelines for ethical decision making. It even has an ethics office and a director of ethics! The most important ethics document at TI is called *Ethics in the Business of TI.*

The spirit of TI's code of ethics is described by the former chairman, president, and chief executive officer, "We will always place integrity before shipping, before billings, before profits, before anything. If it comes down to a choice between making a desired profit and doing it right, we don't have a choice. We'll do it right."[1] The code addresses the marketplace, gifts and entertainment, improper use of corporate assets, political contributions, payments in connection with business transactions, conflict of interest, investment in TI stock, TI proprietary information, trade secrets and software of others, transactions with governmental agencies, and disciplinary action, among other subjects.

Although some companies had already developed codes of ethics, the fallout from the collapse of Enron, and from the similar financial misreporting of other companies, inspired Congress to pass the 2002 Sarbanes-Oxley Act. In addition to addressing numerous issues related to corporate financial reporting, the Act also emphasizes the importance of a code of ethics for companies' financial officers (for example, chief financial officers, controllers, and chief accountants). In fact, the Act directed the Securities and Exchange Commission to require corporations to include a statement in their annual reports about whether or not they adopted a code of ethics for their financial officers, and if not, why not.

In our society, we expect people to behave within a range of civilized standards. This expectation allows our society to function with minimal confusion and misunderstanding. Similarly, accounting information developed in an ethical environment allows our economy to function efficiently, and to direct or allocate our resources productively. In both our personal and our business lives, ethics and integrity are our "social glue."

CREATIVE AND CRITICAL THINKING IN BUSINESS AND ACCOUNTING

9 What are creative and critical thinking?

The business environment is evolving at an increasingly rapid pace. Economic events are complex, ambiguous, dynamic, and difficult to interpret. In this type of environment, companies face challenges for which no guidelines, or only sketchy guidelines, exist. These challenges present opportunities for companies to grow and change. To be successful, decision makers (e.g., owners, managers) must try to anticipate changes in the business environment, to address the associated challenges even before they occur, and to maximize their companies' opportunities to grow and change. In order to make optimum decisions in this environment, these decision makers must develop and use their creative and critical thinking skills to find creative solutions to problems and to identify the best of these solutions. In fact, recognizing a crucial need for people with more of these skills, retail, manufacturing, and service companies, including accounting firms, are actively recruiting "the best and the brightest" creative and critical thinkers.

Creative thinking is the process of actively generating new ideas. Generally, this process refers to spontaneous and free-flowing thoughts that open the door to new ideas. In the context of problem solving and decision making, the object of creative thinking is to generate lots of ideas (fluency) and a broad range of ideas (flexibility) that may result in potential solutions to a problem. **Fluency** refers to the *number* of ideas generated or solutions proposed as problem solutions. **Flexibility** refers to the *spectrum* of ideas generated. Of course, proposing solutions to a problem requires recognition that there is a problem to solve. Accepting, without question, the way things are makes it difficult to get creative about the solution to that problem. Creative thinkers, then, must have a questioning attitude, or inquisitiveness, and must be "problem finders" as well as "idea generators."

Critical thinking is the process that evaluates the ideas generated by creative thinking. Critical thinking determines if any of the ideas will work, what types of problems they might have, whether they can be improved, and which ones are better than others. Critical thinking requires characteristics such as independence and objectivity. Being

independent means that in the process of evaluating ideas, the critical thinker must rely on his or her own conclusions rather than those of others. He or she doesn't accept the beliefs of others without questioning where those ideas came from, what evidence supports them, and what assumptions were made in developing the ideas. **Objectivity** is the quality of being unbiased.

APPLYING CREATIVE AND CRITICAL THINKING TO BUSINESS DECISIONS

10 What are the logical stages in problem solving and decision making?

Many business problems can involve a jumble of information, opinions, considerations, risks, and alternatives. A systematic method, including creative and critical thinking, is necessary to organize the problem-solving approach and to decide on a solution to the problem. Exhibit 1-11 illustrates the four stages in decision making and the particular impact of creative and critical thinking on each stage. Notice that creative thinking is more important in the earlier stages, while critical thinking is more important in the later stages. We will discuss these stages of decision making in the next four sections.

Recognizing and Defining the Problem

The first stage in solving a problem is the recognition and definition of the problem for which a decision must be made. For example, a manager within Unlimited Decadence might be faced with such issues as what selling price to set for a candy bar, whether to introduce a new Empty Decadence (calorie-free) candy bar, or whether to apply for a bank loan, to name a few. As we suggested earlier, the chances of arriving at a successful solution to a problem are considerably reduced if the decision maker does not have a clear understanding of the problem. An incorrectly defined problem will lead to an unproductive course of action at best and could actually create new problems or make the current problem worse. To fully understand the problem, the decision maker needs to gather the facts surrounding the problem, identify the objectives that would be achieved by solving the problem, and clearly state the problem. He or she would use creative thinking skills to brainstorm a list of questions about the problem.

Identifying Alternative Solutions

After the problem has been clearly defined and stated, the decision maker, using both creative and critical thinking, identifies alternative solutions. Generating numerous alternative solutions makes it more likely that at least one will be workable.

Discussing the problem and possible solutions with other people can help identify alternative solutions. By talking with people who are uninvolved with or unaffected by the problem or its solution, the decision maker is likely to get a more objective assessment of the problem or perhaps an entirely new perspective on it. After generating a list of ideas, the decision maker must critically evaluate them to identify potentially workable solutions that fit within the boundaries or limits of the company.

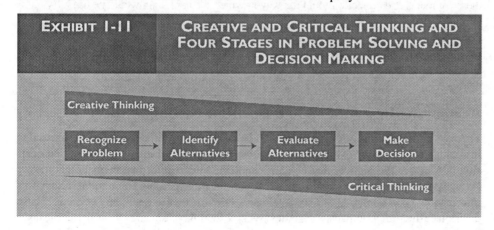

EXHIBIT 1-11 **CREATIVE AND CRITICAL THINKING AND FOUR STAGES IN PROBLEM SOLVING AND DECISION MAKING**

Creative Thinking

Recognize Problem → Identify Alternatives → Evaluate Alternatives → Make Decision

Critical Thinking

Weighing the Advantages and Disadvantages of Each Solution

After identifying potential workable solutions, the decision maker must evaluate each of them. Although creative thinking and critical thinking are both useful in developing a list of the advantages and disadvantages of each solution, critical thinking becomes paramount in this stage.

In the business environment, accounting information is useful in evaluating each solution because each may have different economic effects. Accounting information that is relevant in weighing the advantages and disadvantages of each solution includes information about the solution's effect on the company's costs, profits, and related income taxes, as well as its effect on the timing of cash receipts and payments.

After gathering accounting and other information for each alternative, the decision maker can list and evaluate the advantages and disadvantages of each workable solution in order to fully understand each alternative solution.

Choosing a Solution

The first three stages of the problem-solving process break down the problem in a systematic and detailed manner so that the decision maker becomes completely familiar with the problem and its possible solutions. After these first three stages, he or she must choose the best solution from among the alternative workable solutions, making the decision based, to a great extent, on the accounting information gathered in the previous stage, in which he or she evaluated the alternatives. However, even after the advantages and the disadvantages of each alternative have been listed and quantified (when possible), the choice of a solution can be difficult. This is because individual advantages and disadvantages weigh differently in the decision and are hard to compare. Not all advantages are equally desirable, and not all disadvantages are equally undesirable. One technique that is useful in ordering the alternatives is to rank them based on their effectiveness in achieving the desired results, and then also to rank them based on their desirability in terms of the company's value system. Another technique that is useful in choosing a solution is to combine the best features of multiple alternative solutions while eliminating some of the disadvantages that each alternative would have if it alone was selected.

Notice that creative and critical thinking are used throughout the problem-solving and decision-making process, although not evenly throughout the process. As we illustrated in Exhibit 1-11, some stages of the process require more of one kind of thinking than the other.

The decision-making process is similar for people who are outside the company and are making decisions about the company. For example, assume Unlimited Decadence applies for a bank loan. When this request is made, the banker recognizes that a decision must be made about granting the loan. For the banker, there are many alternatives, including refusing the bank loan, granting a loan of a smaller or greater amount for a shorter or longer time, or granting the loan as requested. The banker must have information concerning the cash in Unlimited Decadence's checking and savings accounts, the cash Unlimited Decadence must spend to pay its bills and the amount it expects to collect from its customers, the timing of these payments and collections, and the way in which the bank loan would be used. By gathering the related accounting information, the banker can evaluate whether Unlimited Decadence needs the bank loan, the appropriate amount and length of time of the loan, and the likelihood that Unlimited Decadence will repay the loan. The banker makes the loan decision, to a great extent, on the basis of accounting information provided by Unlimited Decadence.

Accounting Information and Decision Making

The role of accounting information in the decision-making process is further illustrated in Exhibit 1-12. As this exhibit illustrates, the accounting information system and decision making are *interactive;* that is, an accountant collects information about a company (locates, gathers, interprets, and organizes relevant information) and communicates this information to both internal and external users to assist them in making decisions. These decisions affect the company's activities, which then have an impact on the company's

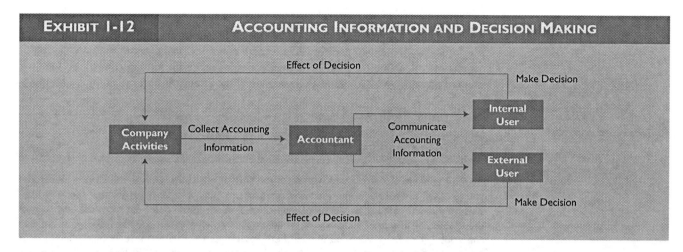

resulting accounting information (as is reflected when the accounting information accumulation and communication process is repeated again).

For the product decisions and bank loan, you can see that the decisions made by both the internal and the external users will affect the accounting information accumulated and communicated about the company. Before either decision is reached, the information accumulated and communicated will be the information needed to make the decisions, as we discussed earlier. After the decisions are made, regardless of the alternative chosen (whether or not Unlimited Decadence manufactures and sells the Empty Decadence candy bar and whether or not the bank grants a loan to Unlimited Decadence), the result of the decision will affect Unlimited Decadence's future activities and, in turn, result in different accounting information about the company.

CREATIVE AND CRITICAL THINKING ORIENTATION OF THE BOOK

In the rapidly changing business environment, the businessperson must interpret, evaluate, synthesize, and apply new information and technology. With this new information and technology come new problems, many of which have several reasonable solutions and many of which may not have obvious solutions or any solutions. In this environment, decision makers are not operating in a "textbook world," where there are clear-cut, right and wrong answers and where the relevant facts for making decisions are neatly laid out. Therefore, to help you prepare for this challenging environment, throughout this book we will illustrate the use of creative and critical thinking for solving accounting-related problems. Then, in the Integrated Business and Accounting Situations at the ends of the chapters, we will give you the opportunity to enhance your own creative and critical thinking skills. In addition to solving problems that have specific "correct" solutions, we will ask you to make decisions and to solve problems that may have several reasonable solutions or obscure solutions. We will also ask you to interpret, evaluate, and synthesize information and to apply new information to new and different situations. In other words, we will be asking you to think creatively and critically.

FRAMEWORK OF THE BOOK

Beginning in Chapter 2 we will discuss, in more depth, accounting and its use in the management activities of planning, operating, and evaluating, starting with a simple company. Then, in later chapters, we will progress through more complex companies. We will also discuss the use of accounting by decision makers outside the company.

As you read through the book, you will begin to notice the same topics reemerging; but note that each time, a topic will be refined or enhanced by a different company structure, a different type of business, or a different user perspective. You will also notice that we continue to discuss ethical considerations. That's because ethical considerations exist in all aspects of business and accounting.

You will also notice that international issues appear again and again. Many companies operating in the United States have home offices, branches, and subsidiaries in other countries or simply trade with companies in foreign countries. Managers must know the implications of conducting business in foreign countries and with foreign companies. External users of accounting information also must know the effects of these business connections.

SUMMARY

At the beginning of the chapter we asked you several questions. During the chapter, we asked you to STOP and answer some additional questions to build your knowledge about specific issues. Be sure you answered these additional questions. Below are the questions from the beginning of the chapter, with a brief summary of the key points relating to the answers. Use your creative and critical thinking skills to expand on these key points to develop more complete answers to the questions and to determine what other questions you have that might lead you to learn more about the issues.

1 Why is it necessary to have an understanding of business before trying to learn about accounting?

Accounting involves identifying, measuring, recording, summarizing, and communicating economic information about a company for decision making. It focuses on the resources and activities of companies. Therefore, you need to understand companies and the business environment in which they exist, before trying to learn how to account for their resources and activities.

2 What is the role of accounting information within the business environment?

Accounting information helps people inside and outside companies make decisions. It supports management activities by providing managers with quantitative information about their company to aid them in planning, operating, and evaluating the company's activities. Accounting information supports external decision making by providing people outside of the company—such as investors, creditors, stockbrokers, financial analysts, bankers, suppliers, labor unions, customers, and governments—with financial statements containing economic information about the performance of the company.

3 What is private enterprise, and what forms does it take?

Companies in the private enterprise system produce goods and services for a profit. These companies can be service, merchandising, or manufacturing companies. Entrepreneurs, or individuals, invest money in companies so that the companies can acquire resources, such as inventory, buildings, and equipment. The companies then use these resources to earn a profit. The three types of business organization are (1) the sole proprietorship, owned by one individual, (2) the partnership, owned by two or more individuals (partners), and (3) the corporation, incorporated as a separate legal entity and owned by numerous stockholders who hold capital stock in the corporation.

4 What types of regulations do companies face?

The activities of companies must be regulated because these activities affect us, other companies, the economy, and the environment. All companies, regardless of type, size, or complexity, must contend with regulatory issues. Numerous laws and authorities regulate companies on issues ranging from environmental protection to taxes. Each city, county, state, and country has its own regulations. Owners of companies must learn and comply with the regulations issued by the governments where the companies are located and in the areas in which the companies conduct business.

5 What activities contribute to the operations of a company?

Managers strive to make their company successful through setting and achieving the goals of their company, making decisions, and committing the resources of the company to the achievement of these goals. Planning provides the organization and direction for the other activities. Operating involves gathering the necessary resources and employees and implementing the plans. Evaluating measures the actual progress against standards or benchmarks so that problems can be corrected.

6 **Are there any guidelines for reporting to company managers?**

The Institute of Management Accountants publishes a broad set of nonbinding guidelines for management accountants to use in fulfilling their responsibilities. These guidelines provide help for management accountants when they are faced with new situations.

7 **Are there any guidelines in the United States for reporting to people outside of a company?**

So that external users can understand the meaning of accounting information, companies follow agreed-upon principles in their external reports. The FASB and SEC contribute to the development of generally accepted accounting principles, the standards or "rules" that many companies must follow.

8 **What role does ethics play in the business environment?**

Since the world is a complex place, where issues are not always clear, decisions must be made in an ethical context with the best available information. Accounting information can be relied on only if it is generated in an ethical environment. Many groups have established codes of ethics.

9 **What are creative and critical thinking?**

Creative thinking is the process of actively generating new ideas. Generally, this process refers to spontaneous and free-flowing thoughts that open the door to new ideas. In the context of problem solving and decision making, the object of creative thinking is to generate lots of ideas and a broad range of ideas that may result in potential solutions to a problem. Critical thinking is the process that evaluates the ideas generated by creative thinking. Critical thinking determines if any of the ideas will work, what types of problems they might have, whether they can be improved, and which ones are better than others.

10 **What are the logical stages in problem solving and decision making?**

Many business problems are difficult and complicated. A systematic approach is necessary to organize the process and to decide on a solution to the problem. The four stages in problem solving and decision making are (1) recognize the problem, (2) identify alternatives, (3) evaluate the alternatives, and (4) make the decision. The accounting information system plays a big part in the business decision-making process.

KEY TERMS

annual report *(p. 19)*

assets *(p. 18)*

balance sheet *(p. 18)*

budgeting *(p. 14)*

capital *(p. 6)*

cash flow statement *(p. 19)*

corporation *(p. 7)*

cost analysis or cost accounting *(p. 14)*

creative thinking *(p. 22)*

critical thinking *(p. 22)*

entrepreneur *(p. 6)*

evaluating *(p. 12)*

expenses *(p. 17)*

external users *(p. 10)*

financial accounting *(p. 15)*

financial statements *(p. 17)*

flexibility *(p. 22)*

fluency *(p. 22)*

generally accepted accounting principles (GAAP) *(p. 16)*

income statement *(p. 17)*

independence *(p. 23)*

integrated accounting system *(p. 10)*

internal users *(p. 10)*

international financial reporting standards *(p. 17)*

liabilities *(p. 18)*

management accounting *(p. 13)*

manufacturing companies *(p. 5)*

merchandising companies *(p. 4)*

net income *(p. 18)*

net loss *(p. 18)*

objectivity *(p. 23)*

operating *(p. 12)*

owner's equity *(p. 18)*

partnership *(p. 7)*

partnership agreement *(p. 7)*

planning *(p. 11)*

profit *(p. 17)*

revenues *(p. 17)*

service companies *(p. 4)*

sole proprietorship *(p. 7)*

solvency *(p. 17)*

solvent *(p. 6)*

statement of changes in owner's equity *(p. 18)*

stockholders' equity *(p. 18)*

SUMMARY SURFING

Here is an opportunity to gather information on the Internet about real-world issues related to the topics in this chapter (for suggestions on how to navigate various organizations' Web sites to find the relevant information, see the related discussion in the Preface at the beginning of the book). Answer the following questions.

- Go to the **Financial Executives Institute** Web site. The FEI's Code of Ethics lists responsibilities that its members have to several groups of people. To what groups is the Code referring? Give an example of a responsibility that members have to each group.

- Go to the resources in the **Foundations of Critical Thinking** Web site and look for articles on the fundamentals of critical thinking. Identify the eight elements of reasoning helpful to students in developing their reasoning abilities. List two activities under each guideline. Which guideline(s) seems especially helpful to you?

- Go to the **Creativity Web** Web site to learn about creativity basics and techniques. What are some obstacles to creativity? What are some of the suggestions given to overcome these obstacles?

APPENDIX

The Profession of Accountancy

Perhaps you are wondering what the profession of accountancy is all about. Accountancy has emerged as a profession, alongside other professions such as medicine, law, and architecture. Two characteristics distinguish a profession from an occupation. One is that its members have exclusive technical competence in their field requiring extensive training and specialized study. These members usually demonstrate their initial competence by taking a standardized exam. The second distinguishing characteristic of a profession is that its members adhere to a service ideal (they render a specialized service to the public) and its supporting standards of conduct and ethics. As we discuss in this appendix, the profession of accountancy meets both of these criteria. First of all, the study and the practice of accountancy require a broad understanding of concepts in such areas as business, economics, sociology, psychology, and public administration, as well as an in-depth technical knowledge of specialized accounting areas. Accountants demonstrate their understanding of these concepts and their technical accounting knowledge by taking standardized exams such as the CPA Exam, the CMA Exam, and the CFE Exam, which we will discuss later. Secondly, accountants render specialized accounting services in four general areas (or fields) and must comply with specific standards of conduct and ethics (as you read about in the main part of this chapter).

The four general fields of accountancy include (1) industry accounting, (2) public accounting, (3) governmental accounting, and (4) education, each of which has several accounting specialty areas. We summarize them in Exhibit 1-13 and discuss them briefly here.

Industry Accounting

A company employs industry, or management, accountants to perform its internal (management) accounting activities and to prepare its financial reports. A high-level manager, such as the company's **controller**, usually coordinates these activities. This manager frequently reports directly to a top manager of the organization, such as the **chief financial officer**—an indication of how important the management accounting functions are to the company's operations.

Another indication of the importance of management accounting is the Certificate in Management Accounting (CMA). The CMA is granted to those who meet specific educational and pro-

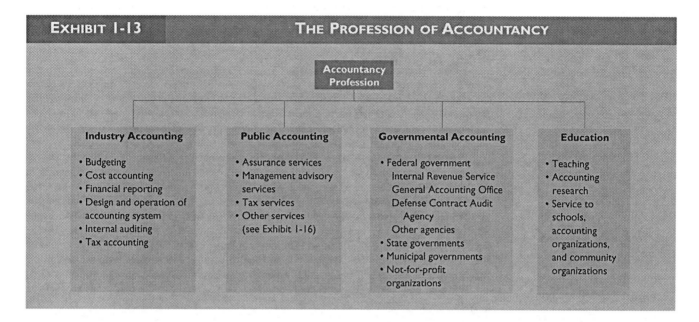

EXHIBIT 1-13		THE PROFESSION OF ACCOUNTANCY	

Accountancy Profession

Industry Accounting	Public Accounting	Governmental Accounting	Education
• Budgeting • Cost accounting • Financial reporting • Design and operation of accounting system • Internal auditing • Tax accounting	• Assurance services • Management advisory services • Tax services • Other services (see Exhibit 1-16)	• Federal government Internal Revenue Service General Accounting Office Defense Contract Audit Agency Other agencies • State governments • Municipal governments • Not-for-profit organizations	• Teaching • Accounting research • Service to schools, accounting organizations, and community organizations

fessional standards and who pass a uniform CMA examination, administered twice yearly by the **Institute of Management Accountants**. Although the CMA is not required as a license to practice, accountants holding the CMA are recognized as professional experts in the area of management accounting.

Management accounting activities encompass several areas: budgeting, cost accounting, and financial reporting (which we discussed briefly in this chapter), as well as designing and operating accounting systems, internal auditing, and tax accounting. We discuss the last three of these areas next.

Design and Operation of an Integrated Accounting System

One duty of the management accountant is to design and operate a company's integrated accounting system, which may be a part of its bigger enterprise resource planning (ERP) system (which we discuss in Chapter 9). This function is sometimes referred to as **general accounting** because of the wide variety of activities involved. These activities include, among others, deciding how much of the accounting system will be computer or manually operated, determining the information needs of different managers and departments, integrating the accounting activities for those departments, and designing accounting procedures, forms, and reports.

Internal Auditing

One part of the design of an accounting system is establishing good internal control. As we discuss in Chapter 8, **internal control** involves the procedures needed to control or minimize a company's risks (of losses, earnings drops, fraud, fines, scandal, and so forth), to safeguard a company's economic resources, and to promote the efficient and effective operation of its accounting system. Internal auditing is a part of a company's internal control procedures and has as its purpose the review of the company's operations to ensure that all company employees are following these procedures. Internal auditing is becoming increasingly important because, as you will see shortly, the procedures for a company's *external* audit depend, to a great degree, on the quality of its internal control. As evidence of professionalism in internal auditing, an accountant may earn a Certificate of Internal Auditing (CIA), awarded by the **Institute of Internal Auditors, Inc.** Although not a license to practice, this certificate states that the holder has met specified educational and practical experience requirements and has passed the uniform CIA examination.

Tax Accounting

Although companies often assign their tax work to the tax services department of a public accounting firm, many of them maintain their own tax departments as well. Accountants with expertise in the tax laws that apply to the company make up the staff of these departments. These accountants handle income tax planning and the preparation of the company's state, federal, and foreign income tax returns. They also work on real estate taxes, personal property taxes (such as taxes on inventories), and other taxes.

Public Accounting

A public accountant is an independent professional who provides accounting services to clients for a fee. Many accountants practice public accounting as individual practitioners or work in local or regional public accounting firms. Others work in large public accounting firms that have offices in most major U.S. and international cities. These firms provide accounting services to large corporations, some of which span the United States as well as the world in their activities.

Most public accountants are **certified public accountants** (CPAs). A CPA has met the requirements of the state in which he or she works, and holds a license to practice accounting in that state. States use licensing as a means of protecting the public interest by helping to ensure that public accountants provide high-quality, professional services. Although the licensing requirements vary from state to state, all CPAs must pass the Uniform CPA Examination. The "CPA exam," which tests the skills and knowledge of entry-level accountants, is a national examination given by the **American Institute of Certified Public Accountants (AICPA)**. Exhibit 1-14 lists the skills and knowledge tested on the CPA exam. In addition to passing the exam, a CPA must have met a state's minimum educational and practical experience requirements to be licensed in that state.

But what do public accountants *do*? Next, we discuss several services that public accountants provide to their client.

Assurance Services

As a result of the information age, the volume of all types of information has grown, and much of that information is readily available to companies, governments, organizations, and individuals. Since decision makers increasingly rely on such information, they need assurance that the information is valid for the purposes for which they intend to use it. In this regard, "an assurance involves expression of a written or oral conclusion on the reliability and/or relevance of information and/or information systems."[2] Auditing evolved from a need for a specific type of assurance service.

Auditing Accounting information is one type of information for which decision makers need assurance. One way a company communicates accounting information is by issuing financial statements. Managers of the company issuing the statements are responsible for preparing these statements. But because of the potential bias of these managers, external users of the financial statements need objective assurance that the statements *fairly* represent the results of the activities of the company. Therefore, both the **New York Stock Exchange** and the **American Stock Ex-**

EXHIBIT 1-14	REVISED CPA EXAM[a]

Content (Knowledge) Areas	Skills Needed to Apply Knowledge
Auditing & Attestation—tests knowledge of auditing procedures, generally accepted auditing standards, and other standards related to attest engagements, and the skills needed to apply that knowledge in those engagements	Ability to communicate
	Ability to perform research
Financial Accounting & Reporting—tests knowledge of generally accepted accounting principles for business enterprises, not-for-profit organizations, and governmental entities, and the skills needed to apply that knowledge	Ability to analyze and organize information
Regulation—tests knowledge of federal taxation, ethics, professional and legal responsibilities, and business law, and the skills needed to apply that knowledge	Ability to understand and apply knowledge from diverse areas
Business Environment & Concepts—tests knowledge of general business environment and business concepts that candidates need to know in order to understand the underlying business reasons for and accounting implications of business transactions, and the skills needed to apply that knowledge	Ability to use judgment

[a]*The Uniform CPA Examination Candidate Bulletin*, June 2009, http://www.nasba.org.

[2]AICPA-sponsored meeting of representatives of small and medium-sized firms, regulators, and scholars.

change, as well as the **Securities and Exchange Commission**, require that the set of financial statements that certain corporations (those offering equity securities for public sale) issue every year be audited. This audited set of financial statements is called an **annual report**. Similarly, a bank may require a company to provide audited financial statements when the company applies for a loan. For the same reason, other types of economic entities, such as universities and charitable organizations, also issue audited financial statements. But what does it mean to be audited?

Auditing involves the examination, by an *independent* CPA, of a company's accounting records and financial statements, and the company's internal control over its financial reporting. This internal control is a process, designed by the company, to help assure that its financial reporting is reliable. Based on sample evidence gathered in the auditing process, including evidence about the quality of the company's internal controls, the CPA forms and expresses a professional, unbiased opinion about (or *attests* to) the fairness of the accounting information in the company's financial statements. The CPA also expresses an opinion about the effectiveness of the company's internal controls. Auditing plays an important role in society because many external users rely on CPAs' opinions when making decisions about whether to engage in activities with companies, universities, charitable organizations, and other economic entities.

Other Assurance Services

Recently, because of their clients' needs for assurance about other types of information, public accounting firms have begun to expand their assurance services. In the interest of helping public accounting firms serve their customers, the AICPA, through one of its committees,[3] identified some specific opportunities for these firms to provide assurance services. Exhibit 1-15 summarizes some of these opportunities.

Management Advisory Services

In addition to auditing departments, many public accounting firms have separate management advisory services departments to conduct special studies to advise non-audit client companies about improving their internal operations and to aid client managers in their various activities. These departments, in part, help to provide some of the assurance services we discussed earlier.

Management advisory services in public accounting firms include the design or improvement of a company's financial accounting system for identifying, measuring, recording, summarizing, and reporting accounting information. These services also may include assistance in areas such as developing cost-control systems, planning manufacturing facilities, and installing computer operations. To provide these services, public accounting firms also must have employees who have a strong understanding of the industries in which their clients operate. Therefore, in addition to hiring accountants, public accounting firms hire people with other specialties—people such as lawyers, industrial engineers, and systems analysts.

Management advisory services in public accounting firms also may include the prevention and detection of fraud within their client companies. This service may include helping these companies understand their vulnerability to potential fraud, identify high-risk areas of the company, develop a prevention plan that addresses the most vulnerable and critical areas, monitor the ongoing

EXHIBIT 1-15	OPPORTUNITIES FOR PROVIDING ASSURANCE SERVICES

- Assessing whether an entity has identified all its risks and is effectively managing them
- Evaluating whether an entity's performance measurement system contains relevant and reliable measures of its progress toward its goals and objectives
- Assessing whether an entity's integrated information system (or its ERP system) provides reliable information for decision making
- Assessing whether systems used in e-commerce provide appropriate data integrity, security, privacy, and reliability
- Assessing the effectiveness of health care services provided by HMOs, hospitals, doctors, and other providers
- Assessing whether various caregivers are meeting specified goals regarding care for the elderly

[3]AICPA Special Committee on Assurance Services.

effectiveness of the plan in preventing or reducing fraud, and respond to actual occurrences of fraud. Many public accountants who work in this area are **certified fraud examiners (CFEs)**. The CFE is awarded by the **Association of Certified Fraud Examiners (ACFE)**. All CFEs must pass the CFE Examination which includes questions about fraud examination and investigation, criminology and ethics, financial transactions, and legal elements of fraud.

Tax Services

The federal government, governments of other countries, and most state governments require corporations and individuals to file income tax returns and to pay taxes. Because of the high tax rates, complex tax regulations, and special tax incentives today, most companies (and individuals) can benefit from carefully planning their activities to minimize or postpone their tax payments. This is called **tax planning**. Many public accounting firms have separate tax services departments that employ tax professionals who are experts in the various federal, foreign government, and state tax regulations. These tax professionals assist companies and individuals in tax planning. In addition to tax planning, the tax services departments of public accounting firms frequently prepare client corporation or individual income tax returns that reflect the results of these tax-planning activities.

Other Services

When clients hire an accountant or an accounting firm, they really are not as interested in reports that look good as they are in good advice, sound thinking, and creative answers to difficult problems. Computers, the Internet, and other recent high-tech developments allow accountants to do less "number crunching" and more advising, thinking, and creating. As a result of client demand, both large and small public accounting firms have expanded the types of services they offer their individual, small and medium-sized companies, and large corporate clients. These services can range from asset valuation to creative financing.

For example, one CPA, a sole practitioner, worked on one of the largest divorce cases in Texas history. He was hired to assign a value to the feuding couple's family-owned baseball card company. Texas is a community property state, and the company had to be sold in the divorce proceedings so the unhappy couple could split the cash received from the sale of the company. By analyzing the company's assets and what they would be worth when sold, and by looking at the company's potential future cash flows and net income, the accountant helped the couple determine the value of the company, which eventually sold for $87.5 million!

Accountants who focus on small companies can help their clients find sources of creative financing. Most new companies have difficulty finding capital to pay for their continued growth. Without a long business history, many of these companies don't qualify for traditional bank loans. Accountants can help these companies locate alternative financing sources, such as asset-based lending, leasing, and loans guaranteed by the Small Business Administration. Exhibit 1-16 lists some additional services that public accountants provide to their clients.

Governmental and Quasi-Governmental Accounting

Certain governmental and quasi-governmental agencies also employ accountants. The Internal Revenue Service, for example, is responsible for the collection of federal income taxes. State revenue agencies also perform similar functions. Administrators of other federal, state, and local government agencies are responsible for the control of both tax revenues and tax expenditures. These agencies hire accountants to provide accounting information for use in the administration of these activities.

Several other governmental organizations also employ accountants. As we mention in this chapter, the **Securities and Exchange Commission** (SEC) is responsible for overseeing the

EXHIBIT 1-16	OTHER SERVICES THAT PUBLIC ACCOUNTANTS PROVIDE FOR THEIR CLIENTS
Estate planning	Business succession planning
Forensic accounting	Debt restructuring and bankruptcy advising
Real estate advisory services	Business planning
Technology consulting	Personal financial planning
Business valuation	E-commerce advising
Merger and acquisition assistance	Environmental accounting
International accounting	

reported financial statements of certain corporations and has the legal authority to establish accounting regulations for them. The SEC employs accountants to identify appropriate accounting standards and to verify that corporations are following existing regulations. The **General Accounting Office (GAO)** is responsible for cooperating with various agencies of the federal government in the development and operation of their accounting systems to improve the management of these agencies. It also oversees the administration of government contracts and the spending of federal funds. The **Defense Contract Audit Agency (DCAA)** audits all federally funded defense contracts. Its work resembles the audit services of public accounting firms. Other federal and state agencies, such as the **Federal Bureau of Investigation**, the **Environmental Protection Agency**, and the **Federal Communications Commission**, also employ accountants to prepare and use accounting information.

Administrators of federal, state, municipal, and other not-for-profit organizations such as colleges and universities, hospitals, and mental health agencies are responsible for their organizations' efficient and effective operations. The accounting information needed by these organizations is similar to that needed by companies. But because they are not-for-profit organizations financed in part by public funds, these organizations are required to use somewhat different accounting procedures (sometimes called *fund accounting*). These organizations hire accountants to design and operate their accounting systems.

As evidence of professionalism in governmental accounting, an accountant may become a Certified Government Financial Manager (CGFM). A CGFM must have met specified educational and practical experience requirements and must have passed a uniform CGFM exam.

THE ACCOUNTANT OF THE 21ST CENTURY

The AICPA has developed a set of core competencies that all college graduates entering the *profession of accountancy* should possess, along with the traditional technical accounting skills they studied in college. It divided these competencies into three categories: *functional competencies* (technical competencies most closely aligned with the value that accounting professionals add to the business environment), *personal competencies* (individual attributes and values), and *broad business perspective competencies* (relating to an understanding of the internal and external business environment). Exhibit 1-17 lists and describes the competencies in each category.

EXHIBIT 1-17	**AICPA CORE COMPETENCIES***

FUNCTIONAL COMPETENCIES relate to the technical competencies, which are most closely aligned with the value contributed by accounting professionals. Functional competencies include:

- Decision Modeling
- Risk Analysis
- Measurement
- Reporting
- Research
- Leverage Technology to Develop and Enhance Functional Competencies

PERSONAL COMPETENCIES relate to the attitudes and behaviors of individuals preparing to enter the accounting profession. Developing these personal competencies will enhance the way professional relationships are handled and facilitate individual learning and personal improvement. Personal competencies include:

- Professional Demeanor
- Problem Solving and Decision Making
- Interaction
- Leadership
- Communication
- Project Management
- Leverage Technology to Develop and Enhance Personal Competencies

BROAD BUSINESS PERSPECTIVE COMPETENCIES relate to the context in which accounting professionals perform their services. Individuals preparing to enter the accounting profession should consider both the internal and external business environments and how their interactions determine success or failure. They must be conversant with the overall realities of the business environment. Broad business perspective competencies include:

- Strategic/Critical Thinking
- Industry/Sector Perspective
- International/Global Perspective
- Resource Management
- Legal/Regulatory Perspective
- Marketing/Client Focus
- Leverage Technology to Develop and Enhance a Broad Business Perspective

* http://www.aicpa.org/edu/corecomp.htm

In order to help accountants acquire the core competencies (or know if they already have these competencies), the **AICPA** also identified the elements (or "sub-competencies") that comprise the competencies, and lists both the competencies and their elements on its web site. Candidates taking the CPA exam are required to demonstrate their ability to apply many of these competencies and elements in all four sections of the exam (in addition to, and in the context of, the traditional accounting skills typically tested on the exam). This ensures that new accountants "have what it takes" to deliver the best services to their clients and to adapt to the ever-changing business environment.

Professional Organizations

A number of *professional* organizations (composed of accounting professionals) exist to facilitate communication among members of the profession, provide professional development opportunities, alert their members to emerging accounting and management issues, and promote ethical conduct. In addition to the Securities and Exchange Commission and the Financial Accounting Standards Board that we mentioned earlier in the chapter, these organizations also influence generally accepted accounting principles (GAAP). Exhibit 1-18 provides a summary of these organizations.

EXHIBIT 1-18	PROFESSIONAL ORGANIZATIONS THAT INFLUENCE GAAP	

Web Site	Organization	Description
http://www.aicpa.org	American Institute of Certified Public Accountants (AICPA)	National professional organization of CPAs. In addition to influencing accounting principles, the AICPA influences auditing standards. The Auditing Standards Board of the AICPA develops auditing standards that govern the way CPAs perform audits. The AICPA also prepares and grades the CPA examination and dispenses the results to the individual states, which then issue licenses to those who have passed the examination and who meet the other qualifications of the state.
http://www.fei.org	Financial Executives Institute (FEI)	Organization of financial executives of major corporations and accounting professors in academia. Examples of member executives include chief financial officers, financial vice-presidents, controllers, treasurers, and tax executives.
http://www.acfe.com	Association of Certified Fraud Examiners (ACFE)	World organization of CFEs. Provides anti-fraud training and education. The ACFE administers the CFE examination.
http://www.imanet.org	Institute of Management Accountants (IMA)	Organization of management accountants and others interested in management accounting. Besides influencing the practice of management accounting, the IMA prepares and grades the CMA examination.
http://www.aaahq.org/index.cfm	American Accounting Association (AAA)	National professional organization of academic and practicing accountants interested in both the academic and research aspects of accounting. Members of the AAA, many of whom are accounting practitioners, influence accounting standard setting through their research on accounting issues.

INTEGRATED BUSINESS AND ACCOUNTING SITUATIONS

Answer the Following Questions in Your Own Words.

Testing Your Knowledge

1-1   How would you describe private enterprise?

1-2   What distinguishes a service company from a merchandising or manufacturing company?

1-3   How is a merchandising company different from a manufacturing company? How are the two types of company the same?

1-4   What is entrepreneurship?

1-5   Suppose you were an entrepreneur. Where might you go for business capital?

1-6   What distinguishes a corporation from a partnership and a sole proprietorship?

1-7   What types of regulations must companies comply with in different jurisdictions?

1-8   What is the purpose of an integrated accounting system?

1-9   Given what you have learned from this chapter, how would you define *accounting?*

1-10   How would you describe the similarities and differences between management accounting and financial accounting? Why are they different and why are they similar?

1-11   How do management accounting reports help managers with their activities?

1-12   What is the purpose of Statements on Management Accounting (SMAs)?

1-13   What are generally accepted accounting principles?

1-14   How do financial accounting reports help external users?

1-15   Why have various business groups found it necessary to establish codes of ethics?

1-16   How do the creative thinking characteristics of fluency and flexibility complement each other?

1-17   What is the difference between being independent and being objective?

1-18   What is the difference between creative thinking and critical thinking? How is each used in decision making and problem solving? How do creative thinking and critical thinking complement each other?

1-19   Describe the stages of problem solving. What pitfalls might you encounter at each stage?

1-20   Describe how accounting information is used in each of the stages of problem solving.

1-21   (Appendix) What does a company's controller do?

1-22   (Appendix) What do you know about an accountant who holds a Certificate in Management Accounting (CMA)?

1-23   (Appendix) What is internal control?

1-24   (Appendix) What is the purpose of internal auditing?

1-25   (Appendix) What do you know about an accountant who holds a Certificate of Internal Auditing (CIA)?

1-26   (Appendix) What are the responsibilities of the accountants who work in a company's tax department?

1-27   (Appendix) What do you know about an accountant who is a certified public accountant (CPA)?

1-28   (Appendix) In addition to knowledge of accounting, what other skills and knowledge prepare a college graduate to enter the profession of accountancy?

1-29   (Appendix) What is an assurance?

1-30   (Appendix) What is auditing?

1-31   (Appendix) What do management advisory services include?

1-32   (Appendix) What tax services does a public accounting firm's tax department perform?

1-33   (Appendix) In addition to assurance services, tax services, and traditional management advisory services, what other services do accountants perform for their clients?

1-34   (Appendix) What different types of jobs might a governmental accountant hold?

1-35   (Appendix) What do you know about an accountant who is a certified government financial manager (CGFM)?

1-36   (Appendix) What are five professional organizations of accountants and who are their members?

Applying Your Knowledge

1-37   How is **American Airlines** an example of a service company? How is **Toyota Motor Corporation** an example of a manufacturing company?

1-38   How might knowledge of a company's cash receipts and payments affect a bank's decision about whether to loan the company money? What financial statement would the loan officer want to look at to begin to understand the company's cash receipts and payments?

1-39   What factors would you consider in deciding whether to operate your company as a sole proprietorship, a partnership, or a corporation?

1-40   Suppose you are Ichabod Cook, CEO of Unlimited Decadence Corporation, maker of candy bars. Unlimited Decadence currently operates in the northeastern United States, and you are considering opening a factory and sales office in California. What questions do you want answered before you proceed with this idea?

1-41   Refer to 1-40. Suppose, instead, that you are considering opening a factory and sales office in Tokyo. What questions do you want answered before proceeding with *this* idea? How do you explain the similarities and differences in these two sets of questions?

1-42   What are some examples of company information in which both internal and external users have an interest?

1-43   Suppose you are a manager of The Foot Note, a small retail store that sells socks. Give an example of information that would help you in each of the management activities of planning, operating, and evaluating the operations of the store.

1-44   What are generally accepted accounting principles, and how do they affect the accounting reports of companies in the United States? Why might the owner or owners of a company be concerned about a proposed new accounting principle?

1-45   A friend of yours, Timorous ("Tim," for short) Ghostly, who has never taken an accounting course, has been assigned a short speech in his speech class. In this speech, Tim must describe the financial statements of a company. Tim has come to you for help (with his professor's permission). He says, "Please describe what financial statements are, what the major financial statements are, and what each financial statement includes." Prepare a written response to Tim's request.

1-46   How do codes of ethics help businesspeople make decisions?

1-47   Suppose that your job is beginning to eat into your personal time. During the last six months you have noticed that you have been taking files home with you to work on after supper and on the weekends. Even so, you are having trouble keeping up. After explaining this to your boss, she suggests that you find a way to work more efficiently. Furthermore, she points out that there are many people who would be glad to take over your job.

Required: (1) What are some alternative ways to approach your boss? What reasons, information, and evidence might support your point of view?

(2) What reasons, information, and evidence might support your boss's point of view? In what ways might these reasons affect the approach you take in presenting your problem to your boss?

1-48   Suppose that your brother, the owner of The Last Custard Stand (a specialty dessert shop), has asked you for a substantial loan to help him expand his business.

Required: What would you like to know about The Last Custard Stand before you make a decision about whether to loan the company money? How could the answers to each of your questions affect your decision? What accounting information could your brother provide you that could affect your decision?

1-49   Refer to 1-48. At your request, your brother provides you with the following information:

Revenues for 2011	$80,000
Expenses for 2011	(65,000)
Profit for 2011	$15,000

Required: How could this information be presented differently to make it more meaningful for you in reaching your loan decision? What could be added to this particular information to make it more meaningful for you?

1-50 The office copier has just quit working and is beyond repair. The big question now is what to do with it. Your boss is offering a cash prize for each of the following:
(a) The longest list of ideas for what to do with the copier
(b) The most unusual idea
(c) The widest variety of ideas

Required: See if you can win all the cash by providing a written list of your ideas.

Making Evaluations

1-51 Your friend, Vito Guarino (an incredible cook!), plans to open a restaurant when he graduates from college. One evening, while extolling the virtues of linguini to you and some of your other friends, he glances down at your accounting textbook, which is open to Exhibit 1-2. "What kind of a company is a restaurant?" he asks. "How would a restaurant fit into this exhibit?" Everyone in the room waits with great anticipation for your answer and the rationale behind your answer. What are you going to say?

1-52 You and your cousin, Harvey, have decided to form a partnership and open a landscaping company in town. But before you do, you and Harvey would like to "iron out" a few details about how to handle various aspects of the partnership and then write a partnership agreement outlining these details. What specific issues would you like to see addressed in the partnership agreement before you begin your partnership with Harvey?

1-53 Suppose you are thinking about whether presidents of companies should be allowed to serve on the FASB. What do you think are the potential benefits of allowing them to serve? What do you think are the potential problems?

1-54 Read a daily newspaper for the next week. What evidence do you find that supports the need for business codes of ethics?

1-55 Is a business suit the most appropriate article of clothing to wear to a business meeting?

Required: Answer the question based on what you believe to be true (answer either "yes," "no," or "not sure"). Explain why you answered the way you did. Now give the reasons and evidence that you believe support your answer (authorities, references, facts, personal experience).

1-56 Consider the plight of the manager at Unlimited Decadence Corporation, whose boss wants to manufacture and sell the new Empty Decadence candy bar, perhaps using it to replace the Decadent Thunderbolt candy bar. Suppose the accounting department has projected that profit per candy bar will be $0.10 higher for the Decadent Thunderbolt than for the Empty Decadence candy bar. The marketing department predicts that Unlimited Decadence can sell 100,000 Empty Decadence candy bars the first year and then more each year for the next ten years if it drops the Decadent Thunderbolt candy bar. During that same time period, the marketing department forecasts that sales of the Decadent Thunderbolt will be 80,000 candy bars the first year, with sales decreasing slightly after that if the company does not produce the Empty Decadence candy bar. However, if the company produces both candy bars, predicted sales for Empty Decadence will be reduced to 70,000 candy bars the first year, with a slow and steady increase in sales over the next ten years. Predicted sales for the Decadent Thunderbolt will decrease to 65,000 during the first year and decrease slightly each year for the next ten years.

The production department has determined that the new candy bar is possible to manufacture and that the factory can be reconfigured to accommodate the new candy bar while continuing to produce the old candy bar. If Unlimited Decadence drops the Decadent Thunderbolt candy bar, it can convert the equipment so that it can be used to produce the Empty Decadence candy bar. The human resources department is confident that numerous qualified people are available to work if the company wants to produce both candy bars. If the company drops the Decadent Thunderbolt candy bar, those people currently working on the Decadent Thunderbolt candy bar can be easily retrained to work on the Empty Decadence candy bar. The chief financial officer has arranged for financing, if it is needed.

Required: (1) Based on the above information, what are the advantages and disadvantages of (a) dropping the Decadent Thunderbolt product line and producing the Empty Decadence candy bar, (b) continuing production of the Decadent Thunderbolt and not producing the Empty Decadence candy bar, (c) producing both the Decadent Thunderbolt and the Empty Decadence candy bars, or (d) producing neither candy bar? How would you decide which alternative is best?

(2) What additional information would make your decision easier?

(3) What other alternative solutions can you think of?

1-57   You just nabbed a plum job joining a team of consultants writing an advice column, "Dear Dr. Decisive," for the local newspaper. Yesterday, you received your first letter:

DR. DECISIVE

Dear Dr. Decisive:

Yesterday, my boyfriend and I got into a high-spirited "discussion" about lucky people in business. I say that most successful businesspeople are just plain lucky. They've been in the right place at the right time. He says that these successful people have worked hard preparing themselves for the time when they will be in the right place at the right time. OK, I think we're saying the same thing. He says there is an important difference. Now he won't call me unless I admit I'm wrong (which I'm not) or until you say I'm right.

I'm right, right?

Call me "Lucky."

Required: Meet with your Dr. Decisive team and write a response to "Lucky."

ENDNOTES

[a]U.S. Treasury Department, Internal Revenue Service, *Statistics of Income Bulletin*, Spring 2009, pp. 200, 201, 204.

[b]Ibid.

[c]Ibid.

[d]Ibid.

[e]Institute of Management Accountants, *Statements on Management Accounting*, http://www.imanet.org/publications_statements.asp.

[f]http://specials.ft.com/enron

[g]*Fortune* magazine, January 10, 2001, pp. 82–110.

[h]Woellert, L., BusinessWeek online, June 1, 2005.

[i]American Institute of Certified Public Accountants, *Code of Professional Conduct*, http://www.aicpa.org.

[j]Institute of Management Accountants, *Statement of Ethical Professional Practice*, http://www.imanet.org/about_ethics_statement.asp..

[k]International Federation of Accountants, *Code of Ethics for Professional Accountants*, http://www.ifac.org.

[l]Texas Instruments Incorporated, *Values and ethics of TI*, http://www.ti.com/corp/docs/csr/corpgov/ethics/ValuesandEthicsofTI/commitment.shtml.

PART 1

PLANNING IN AN ENTREPRENEURIAL ENVIRONMENT

This section includes two chapters that discuss planning for a small company. After reading these chapters, you will be able to:

- *describe what a business plan is and what it contains*

- *prepare various parts of a business plan*

- *understand the differences between variable and fixed costs*

- *use cost-volume-profit analysis in business decisions*

- *prepare a master budget for a retail company*

- *use a master budget in evaluating a company's performance*

DEVELOPING A BUSINESS PLAN: COST-VOLUME-PROFIT ANALYSIS

"HE WHO EVERY MORNING PLANS THE TRANSACTION OF THE DAY, AND FOLLOWS OUT THAT PLAN, CARRIES A THREAD THAT WILL GUIDE HIM THROUGH THE MAZE OF THE MOST BUSY LIFE. BUT WHERE NO PLAN IS LAID, WHERE THE DISPOSAL OF TIME IS SURRENDERED MERELY TO THE CHANCE OF INCIDENCE, CHAOS WILL SOON REIGN."

—VICTOR HUGO

1. Since the future is uncertain and circumstances are likely to change, why should a company bother to plan?

2. What should a company include in its business plan?

3. How does accounting information contribute to the planning process?

4. What must decision makers be able to predict in order to estimate profit at a given sales volume?

5. How can decision makers predict the sales volume necessary for estimated revenues to cover estimated costs?

6. How can decision makers predict the sales volume necessary to achieve a target profit?

7. How can decision makers use accounting information to evaluate alternative plans?

Suppose your sister Anna has hired you, as an employee-advisor, to help her open and run a candy store. Anna, who earned her degree last year with a major in marketing, has an insatiable sweet tooth and has always "hungered" to own a candy store. After long and lively discussions with you about the name of the company, Anna decides to name it "Sweet Temptations." You and Anna arrange to obtain retail space, to purchase display fixtures, supplies, and candy, to hire an employee to sell candy, and to advertise in the newspaper. Now you are ready to open for business. But whoa! Not so fast. Have you thought of everything? If you and Anna want Sweet Temptations to succeed, there are other issues that you must consider before you open your company. Instead of rushing into business when the idea is fresh, first you would be smart to develop a detailed business plan that addresses these issues.

1 Since the future is uncertain and circumstances are likely to change, why should a company bother to plan?

PLANNING IN A NEW COMPANY

Planning is an ongoing process for successful companies. It begins before a company opens for operations and continues throughout the life of the company. A **business plan** is an evolving report that describes a company's goals and its current plans for achieving those goals. The business plan is used by both internal and external users. A business plan typically includes

2 What should a company include in its business plan?

1. a description of the company,
2. a marketing plan,
3. an operating plan,
4. a financial plan.

We will discuss each of these parts in later sections.

A business plan has three main purposes. First, it helps an entrepreneur to visualize and organize the company and its operations. Thinking critically about your hopes for the business and putting a plan on paper will help you and Anna imagine how the plan will work and will help you evaluate the plan, develop new ideas, and refine the plan. By looking at the plan from different points of view, such as those of managers who have responsibility for marketing the company's products or purchasing its inventory of products, you can discover and correct flaws before implementing the plan. Then "paper mistakes" won't become real mistakes!

Second, a business plan serves as a "benchmark," or standard, against which the entrepreneur can later measure the actual performance of a company. You and Anna will be able to evaluate differences between the planned performance of Sweet Temptations, as outlined in its business plan, and its actual performance. Then you will be able to use the results of your evaluation to adjust Sweet Temptations' future activities. For instance, suppose in its first month of business, sales are higher than you and Anna predicted. If you decide that sales will continue at this level, you can use this information to increase Sweet Temptations' future candy purchases.

Third, a business plan helps an entrepreneur obtain the financing that new and growing companies often need. When Anna starts looking for additional funding for Sweet Temptations, potential investors and creditors may request a copy of the company's business plan to help them decide whether or not to invest in Sweet Temptations or to loan it money. For example, as part of its loan-making decisions, **Central Bank** in Jefferson City, Missouri, routinely evaluates the business plans of companies that apply for business loans at the bank.

Investors and creditors, such as Central Bank, have two related concerns when they are making investment and credit decisions. One concern is the level of risk involved with their decisions. **Risk** usually refers to how much uncertainty exists about the future operations of the company. The other concern is the **return,** or money back, that they will receive from their investment and credit decisions. A thorough business plan will provide useful information for helping investors and creditors evaluate their risk and potential return. Now let's look at the parts of a business plan.

Description of the Company

A business plan usually begins with a description of the company and its basic activities. Details of this description include information about the organization of the company, its product or service, its current and potential customers, its objectives, where it is located, and where it conducts its business.

For example, Sweet Temptations is a new retailing company located in a "high-growth" suburb north of a major metropolitan area. Initially, Sweet Temptations will sell only one kind of candy—boxes of chocolates. You and your sister Anna will expand the "product line" to include other kinds of candy as the company grows. After the sale of chocolates is "up and running," and after you graduate, you plan to join Anna full-time as a partner in the company. You and Anna are eager to begin marketing and operating the company but are waiting to do so until after you finish writing the company's business plan and obtain financing. You realize that writing the plan is helping you to think through the various aspects of the business so that you don't "miss something" important in planning your activities. Exhibit 2-1 illustrates how you might describe Sweet Temptations in its business plan.

The organization of a company and its personnel can have a major influence on the success of a company. Therefore, the description of the company also includes a listing of the important people and the major roles they will play in the company. This listing can include the individuals responsible for starting the company, significant investors who

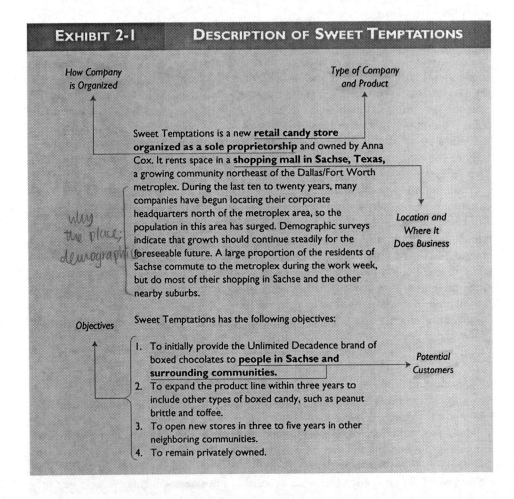

EXHIBIT 2-1   DESCRIPTION OF SWEET TEMPTATIONS

How Company is Organized

Type of Company and Product

Sweet Temptations is a new **retail candy store organized as a sole proprietorship** and owned by Anna Cox. It rents space in a **shopping mall in Sachse, Texas,** a growing community northeast of the Dallas/Fort Worth metroplex. During the last ten to twenty years, many companies have begun locating their corporate headquarters north of the metroplex area, so the population in this area has surged. Demographic surveys indicate that growth should continue steadily for the foreseeable future. A large proportion of the residents of Sachse commute to the metroplex during the work week, but do most of their shopping in Sachse and the other nearby suburbs.

Location and Where It Does Business

Objectives

Sweet Temptations has the following objectives:

1. To initially provide the Unlimited Decadence brand of boxed chocolates to **people in Sachse and surrounding communities.**
2. To expand the product line within three years to include other types of boxed candy, such as peanut brittle and toffee.
3. To open new stores in three to five years in other neighboring communities.
4. To remain privately owned.

Potential Customers

EXHIBIT 2-2	ORGANIZATION OF SWEET TEMPTATIONS

The team at Sweet Temptations is composed of four people, one of whom is a financial consultant. The members of this team are as follows:

Anna Cox	Owner	*Listing of Important*
(Your name)	Employee/adviser	*People and the Roles*
Jaime Gonzales	Employee	*They Will Play*
Joe Smiley	Consultant	

Each of these individuals brings special skills to Sweet Temptations. Anna Cox graduated last year with a B.B.A. in marketing from State U. She has already earned a reputation for her marketing and business skills. While in school, she won the National Student Marketing Association's prestigious Student Marketer of the Year Award and the coveted Small Business Institute's Rising Star Award. She graduated with highest honors. While in school, Anna worked for three retail stores, two of which were start-up companies. One of the start-up companies was a candy store.

(Your name) is an honors business student at State U. and will be graduating in two years. (Your first name) has worked twenty hours per week "keeping the books" at a local candy store for the past two years. Prior to that, (your first name) worked summers and part time during the school year doing miscellaneous jobs at the same candy store.

Qualifications of Important People

Jaime Gonzales is an honors business student at State U. Jaime has worked summers at several restaurants in Sachse.

Joe Smiley is a partner in the management advisory services area of (name of company), a large public accounting firm in Dallas. His firm specializes in consulting with start-up companies.

also are providing expertise and direction to the company, and influential employees and consultants who have a strong impact on the company. Exhibit 2-2 shows some highlights of how you might discuss Sweet Temptations' organization in its business plan. Notice how this part of the plan highlights the combination of your major in business and Anna's degree in marketing. This part may also contain the company's policies or strategies for selecting, training, and rewarding employees. These issues are particularly important for the long-term success of the company.

Marketing Plan

The marketing section of a business plan shows how the company will make sales and how it will influence and respond to market conditions. This section receives a lot of attention from investors and creditors because the company's marketing strategy and its ability to implement that strategy can be very important to the company's success.

The marketing section provides evidence of the demand for the company's products or services, including any market research that has been conducted. This section also describes the current and expected competition in the market, as well as relevant government regulations. The marketing section describes how the company will promote, price, and distribute its products (the company's "marketing strategy"), as well as the predicted growth, market share, and sales of its products (its "sales forecast") by period. This information is helpful to the entrepreneur as a starting point for thinking about the company's other activities related to sales, such as timing the purchase of its inventories. The marketing section is also helpful to people outside the company, such as bank loan officers, because it shows how well the entrepreneur has thought through the company's sales potential and how the company will attract and sell to customers.

Sweet Temptations' business plan may be an inch thick! We don't have room to show each part of its plan, so in the next sections we will ask you to think about what to include. The following is a brief description of Sweet Temptations' market conditions. Initially, Sweet Temptations will have a temporary marketing advantage. Currently, community members must drive at least 30 miles to purchase boxes of Unlimited Decadence chocolates (and they actually make the drive!). After evaluating the community's available retail space (and plans for building retail space), you and Anna believe that there will be very little competition during the next several years. However, you eventually expect competing stores to open in the community. In the meantime, part of your marketing plan is to build a reputation for friendly service and quality products. Your advertising will focus on the quality ingredients used in the chocolates. Furthermore, your initial advertising "punch" will include the fact that Unlimited Decadence now produces, and Sweet Temptations sells, mini-versions of "everyone's favorite candy bars" in boxed form. You believe Sweet Temptations has a distinct advantage in selling Unlimited Decadence chocolates because of the already-established good reputation and popularity of the Unlimited Decadence candy bars.

 What information about market conditions facing Sweet Temptations would you include in the marketing section of its business plan?

Operating Plan

Since a company is organized to deliver a product or service to a market, the business plan must address how the company will develop and enhance its products or services. The company operations section of a business plan includes a description of the relationships between the company, its suppliers, and its customers, as well as a description of how the company will develop, service, protect, and support its products or services. This section also includes any other influences on the operations of the company. The company operations section of the business plan is important because it helps the entrepreneur think through the details of making the idea work. Also, it helps outside users evaluate the entrepreneur's ability to successfully carry out the idea.

Here is a brief description of Sweet Temptations' operations. Sweet Temptations has a ready supply of chocolates. Unlimited Decadence has no sales agreements with any other candy stores within a 30-mile radius of Sweet Temptations. Furthermore, you know of other potential suppliers—candy manufacturers who have high production standards, quality ingredients, and good reputations in the candy industry. In fact, Anna is now talking with representatives of these companies and visiting their kitchens so that she will have identified and selected other suppliers by the time Sweet Temptations is ready to sell other types of candy.

 What information about Sweet Temptations' operations would you include in its business plan?

Other influences on the operations of the company might also be described in this section. These other influences might include the availability of employees, concerns of special-interest groups, regulations, the impact of international trade, and the need for patents, trademarks, and licensing agreements.

If Sweet Temptations' major supplier of chocolates was a company in Brussels, Belgium, rather than Unlimited Decadence Corporation, what additional issues do you think should be included in this section of the business plan? What else do you think managers, owners, creditors, and investors would like to know?

Financial Plan

Since Sweet Temptations is a new company, it has no credit history or recent financial statements. Therefore, Anna should also provide a detailed, realistic financial plan in Sweet Temptations' business plan. The purpose of the financial plan section is to identify the company's capital requirements and sources of capital, as well as to describe the company's projected financial performance. For a new company, this section also highlights the company's beginning financial activities, or "start-up" costs.

Here is some information about Sweet Temptations' start-up costs:

> Anna has decided that she will invest $15,000 of her own money as capital to run Sweet Temptations. Based on the rent charged for space in the shopping mall, she has determined that it will cost $1,000 per month to rent store space in the mall. When Sweet Temptations signs a rental contract for the store in December 2010, it will pay six months' rent in advance, totaling $6,000. Based on a supplier's cost quotation, Anna has determined that Sweet Temptations can buy store equipment for $1,800. The supplier will allow Sweet Temptations to make a $1,000 down payment and to sign a note (a legal document, referred to as a *note payable*) for the remaining amount, to be paid later. Based on the purchases budget (which we will discuss in Chapter 3), Sweet Temptations will purchase 360 boxes of chocolates for "inventory" in December 2010 at a cost of $1,620 from Unlimited Decadence. Unlimited Decadence has agreed to allow Sweet Temptations to pay for this inventory in January 2011. Sweet Temptations will also purchase $700 of supplies in December 2010, paying for the supplies at that time.

What information about Sweet Temptations' start-up costs would you include in the financial section of its business plan?

Identifying Capital Requirements

Most companies eventually need additional funding, or **capital**. The financial section of a business plan should include a discussion of the company's capital requirements and potential sources of that capital. For new companies and small companies, this discussion can be the most important part of the business plan. As you may have noticed while reading the business section of your local newspaper, if a company does not have enough capital and sources of capital, it will have a difficult time surviving.

An entrepreneur can determine a company's capital requirements by analyzing two major issues. First, the entrepreneur should decide what resources the company needs, such as buildings, equipment, and furniture. Then, the entrepreneur can estimate how much capital the business will need in order to acquire those resources. Cost quotations, appraisals, and sales agreements are a good starting point for this estimate. Next, the entrepreneur should analyze the company's projected cash receipts and payments to determine whether it will have enough cash to buy the resources and, if not, how much cash the company will need to borrow. Planning capital requirements involves projections, not guarantees, so the entrepreneur must expect and provide for reasonable deviations from plans. Suppose, for example, that cash sales for the month turn out to be less than expected. For "surprises" like this, the entrepreneur should plan to have a "cash buffer," which is extra cash on hand above the projected short-run cash payments of the company. One purpose of this buffer is to protect the company from differences between actual cash

Significant "start-up" costs for a company.

flows and projected cash flows, and also from unanticipated problems such as having to replace a refrigerated display case sooner than expected. A cash buffer lets the company operate normally through downturns without having to look for financing. It also lets the company take advantage of unexpected opportunities that require cash.

 Can you think of an example of an unexpected opportunity for which an entrepreneur or manager might find a cash buffer to be handy?

Sources of Capital

Once the entrepreneur knows the company's capital requirements, potential sources of capital can be identified. Here, the entrepreneur must know both the length of time that the company plans to use the capital before paying it back to creditors or returning it to investors, and the availability of short- and long-term sources of capital. The entrepreneur can determine how long the company will need to use the capital by analyzing the company's projected cash receipts and payments. We will discuss the tools of this analysis more thoroughly in Chapter 3.

Short-term capital will be repaid within a year or less. Short-term capital can come from two sources. First, suppliers provide short-term capital to some of their customers through what is called "trade credit." Trade credit involves allowing a customer to purchase inventory "on credit" if the customer agrees to pay soon, usually within 30 days. You and Anna have an arrangement with Unlimited Decadence that will allow Sweet Temptations to buy boxed chocolates on credit and pay Unlimited Decadence 30 days later.

 If Sweet Temptations took longer than 30 days, on the average, to sell its inventory of chocolates, do you think its arrangement with Unlimited Decadence would be valuable? What other questions would you like answered to help you determine the answer to this question?

Second, financial institutions, such as commercial banks, provide loans to companies, many of which are guaranteed by government agencies such as the <u>U.S. Small Business Administration</u>. These institutions require a more formal agreement with a company than do issuers of trade credit. Also, they charge interest on these short-term loans. At some point, Anna may talk with her banker to arrange a small line of credit for Sweet Temptations. A **line of credit** allows a company to borrow money "as needed," with a prearranged, agreed-upon interest rate and a specific payback schedule. We discuss short-term capital more in Chapter 8.

Long-term capital will be repaid to creditors or returned to investors after more than a year. Initially, as we mentioned in Chapter 1, companies obtain capital from the owner and from bankers. Sweet Temptations obtained its initial capital from Anna, who invested money from her savings account. Other sources of long-term capital can include friends and relatives, commercial banks, and leasing companies. Many loans are guaranteed by the Small Business Administration or the state's economic-development agency. For example, the owner of **U.S. Resource Recycling Inc.,** a Fontana, California company recently expanded his company into foreign markets. U.S. Resource Recycling purchases materials such as paper products, which are then recycled and sold as exports to some of the company's primary markets in South Korea, Japan, Taiwan, and China. The company received an SBA-guaranteed loan in excess of $750,000 to fuel its expansion. The loan provided funds that allowed the company to add crushing and compression equipment, and to provide cash for the purchase of materials.[a]

 All institutions require a formal agreement with the company about payment dates and interest rates. But suppose Sweet Temptations borrows money from Anna's and your friends and relatives. Do you think it is necessary to have a formal written agreement between these friends and relatives and Sweet Temptations? Why or why not?

Eventually, as a company grows too large to be financed by the owner and these other sources, it may offer private placements or public offerings. Private placements are securities that are sold directly to private individuals or groups (called *investors*). Public offerings involve issuing bonds or stocks to the public (investors) through securities firms or investment bankers. We will discuss bonds and stocks as a source of long-term capital in Chapters 21 and 23 of Volume 2.

For the near future, several of Anna's and your friends and relatives have agreed to lend Sweet Temptations specific amounts of money, as needed. Anna and these friends and relatives have agreed that the interest rate on these loans will match the market interest rate at the time of each loan. Sweet Temptations includes this information in its financial plan.

Projected Financial Performance

This section of the financial plan projects the company's financial performance. Suppose Anna has assigned you the responsibility of preparing this section of Sweet Temptations' financial plan. Although projecting a company's financial performance involves uncertainty, if you follow some guidelines, the financial performance information will be more dependable.

First, the data that you use should be as reliable as possible. Since Sweet Temptations is a new company, you don't have historical data to use for planning purposes. When you have sketchy data (or no data at all), industry averages found in such sources as *Moody's, Standard & Poor's,* and *Robert Morse Associates* can serve as a guide.

 If you use Moody's, Standard & Poor's, or Robert Morse Associates for industry information, you must be able to identify the industry in which Sweet Temptations is operating. What are some key words that you could use to identify the industry?

Second, because predicting a company's financial performance is uncertain, you should consider several scenarios. "What if" questions are useful for this type of planning. What if we sell only 800 boxes of chocolates? What if we sell 1,300 boxes of chocolates? The scenarios should be realistic and perhaps should consider the best case, the worst case, and the most probable case.

Third, you should revise your projection as more facts become available. Finally, it is important that the financial plan is consistent with the information in the other sections of the business plan. For example, since the marketing section of Sweet Temptations' business plan refers to the advertising that you plan to do, the financial plan section must show advertising costs.

The financial performance section of the financial plan includes projected financial statements,[1] supported by cost-volume-profit analysis and budgets. Budgets include reports on such items as estimated sales, purchases of inventory, and expenses, as well as estimated cash receipts and payments. In the remainder of this chapter we will discuss cost-volume-profit analysis and its relationship to the projected income statement. In Chapter 3, we will discuss budgets and how they fit into a company's financial plan.

In summary, you have just learned that the business plan shows the direction a company will be taking during the next year. You have also learned that the business plan includes a description of the company, a marketing plan, an operating plan, and a financial plan. Accountants are most involved with the financial plan, which includes an analysis of predicted costs, sales volumes, and profits. We thus will spend the remainder of this chapter discussing cost-volume-profit analysis and its use in planning.

COST-VOLUME-PROFIT (C-V-P) PLANNING

③ How does accounting information contribute to the planning process?

Determining if a company will be profitable is difficult before it begins operations. This uncertainty is part of the risk that the entrepreneur takes in starting a business. Although it can be scary, it is also part of the fun. Uncertain profit does not mean that the entrepreneur should disregard any type of analysis before beginning the operations of a company, however. It is possible to take educated risks based on estimations of costs, sales volumes, and profits. The financial plan should include an analysis of these factors. One type of analysis that uses these three factors is called *cost-volume-profit analysis*.

Cost-Volume-Profit Analysis

Cost-volume-profit (C-V-P) analysis shows how profit will be affected by alternative sales volumes, selling prices of products, and various costs of the company. C-V-P analysis sometimes is called "break-even analysis." Entrepreneurs use C-V-P analysis to help them understand how the plans they make will affect profits. This understanding can produce more-informed decisions during the ongoing planning process.

C-V-P analysis is based on a simple profit computation involving revenues and costs. This computation can be shown in an equation or in a graph. Although equations provide precise numbers, C-V-P graphs provide a convenient visual form for presenting the analysis to decision-makers. However, to understand a C-V-P equation or graph, decision makers also must understand how costs behave.

Cost Behavior

A careful cost analysis considers the activity level of the operation that causes the cost. For example, Unlimited Decadence, a manufacturing company, might measure its activity by using the number of cases of chocolate bars produced or the number of hours worked in producing these cases of chocolate bars. On the other hand, Sweet Temptations, a retail company, might measure its activity by using the number of boxes of chocolates *sold*. The activity level (the number of boxes of candy bars sold) is often referred to as **volume**. The relationship between an activity's cost and its volume helps us determine the cost's behavior pattern.

To understand what C-V-P equations and graphs reveal about a company's potential profitability, let's first look at two cost behavior patterns that describe how most costs behave. These are called *fixed costs* and *variable costs*.

---

[1]The financial plan usually includes a projected balance sheet, but to simplify the discussion in this chapter, we won't discuss the projected balance sheet until Chapter 11.

Fixed Costs

Fixed costs are constant *in total* for a specific time period; they are *not* affected by differences in volume during that same time period. Managers' annual salaries are usually fixed costs, for instance. For another example, think about the $1,000 monthly rent that Sweet Temptations will pay for its retail space. Sweet Temptations' activity level is its sales volume—the number of boxes of chocolates sold. The rent cost of the retail space will not change as a result of a change in the sales volume, assuming you have planned carefully and have leased enough retail space. Sweet Temptations will pay its monthly rent of $1,000 no matter how many candy bars it sells that month. Since the rent cost does not change as volume changes, it is a fixed cost. The graph in Exhibit 2-3 illustrates the relationship between the rent cost and the sales volume. As you can see, the rent cost will be $1,000 whether Sweet Temptations sells 500 boxes of chocolates or 1,000 boxes.

Note in Exhibit 2-3 that we show a fixed cost as a horizontal straight line on the graph, indicating that the cost will be the same (fixed) over different volume levels. It is important not to be misled about fixed costs. Saying that a cost is "fixed" does not mean that it cannot change from one time period to the next. In the next period, Sweet Temptations could rent more retail space if needed or the landlord could raise the rent when the lease is renewed, causing the rent cost to be higher. To be fixed, a cost must remain constant for a time period in relation to the volume attained *in that same time period.* For example, most companies consider the costs of using their buildings, factories, office equipment, and furniture—called *depreciation*[2]—to be fixed. That is, depreciation costs within a specific time period will not change even if volume changes within that time period.

You have estimated that Sweet Temptations' monthly fixed costs will include the $1,000 rent cost plus $2,050 total salaries for you and Jaime Gonzales (the employee Anna hired to sell candy), $200 consulting costs, $305 advertising costs, $30 supplies costs, $15 depreciation of the store equipment, and $250 telephone and utilities costs.[3] Sweet Temptations' total fixed costs will be the sum of the individual fixed costs, or $3,850.

 What would the graph look like for Sweet Temptations' $3,850 total fixed costs? Why?

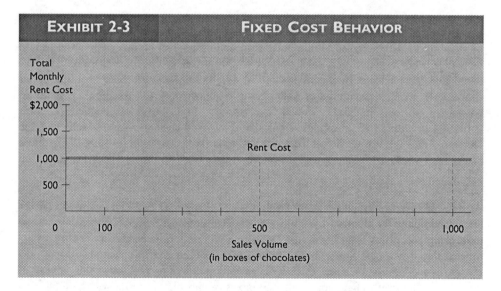

EXHIBIT 2-3	FIXED COST BEHAVIOR

---

[2]We will discuss in Chapters 4 and 20 (of Volume 2) how a company determines its depreciation cost. We include a brief discussion here because most companies have some depreciation costs to consider in evaluating their operations.

[3]Some supplies, telephone, and utility costs may have minimum charges, but their total costs are affected by changes in the volume of usage. These costs are called *mixed costs,* which we will discuss in Chapter 10. For simplicity, here we assume they are fixed costs.

If this box of chocolates contained more pieces of candy, would the company's total fixed costs decrease?

© GETTY IMAGES, INC./PHOTODISC

Decision makers sometimes state fixed costs as a dollar amount *per unit,* computed by dividing total fixed costs by the volume in units. This can be misleading and should be avoided. For instance, at a sales volume of 500 boxes of chocolates, Sweet Temptations' fixed cost per box of chocolates will be $7.70 ($3,850 fixed costs ÷ 500 boxes of chocolates). At a sales volume of 1,000 boxes of chocolates, the fixed cost per box of chocolates will only be $3.85 ($3,850 fixed costs ÷ 1,000 boxes of chocolates). Comparing $7.70 with $3.85, you might think that total fixed costs decrease as sales volume increases. This is not true! Sweet Temptations' total fixed costs will be $3,850 regardless of the sales volume.

Variable Costs

A **variable cost** is constant *per unit* of volume, and changes in total in a time period in direct proportion to the change in volume. For instance, consider Sweet Temptations' cost of purchasing chocolates from Unlimited Decadence to resell to its customers. You have estimated that it will cost Sweet Temptations $4.50 for each box of chocolates that it purchases. The *total cost* of boxes of chocolates sold varies in proportion to the *number* of boxes sold. If Sweet Temptations sells 500 boxes of chocolates in January, the total variable cost of these boxes of chocolates sold will be $2,250 (500 boxes of chocolates × $4.50 per box). If the volume doubles to 1,000 boxes of chocolates, the total variable cost of boxes of chocolates sold will also double to $4,500 (1,000 boxes of chocolates × $4.50 per box). It is important to remember that the total variable cost for a time period increases in proportion to volume in that same time period because each unit has the same variable cost.

Exhibit 2-4 shows the estimated total variable costs of boxes of chocolates sold by Sweet Temptations at different sales volumes. Note that total variable costs are shown by a straight line sloping upward from the origin of the graph. This line shows that the total variable cost increases as volume increases. If no boxes of chocolates are sold, the total variable cost will be $0. If 500 boxes of chocolates are sold, the total variable cost will be $2,250. The slope of the line is the rate at which the total variable cost will increase each time Sweet Temptations sells another box of chocolates. This rate is the variable cost per unit of volume, or $4.50 per each additional box of chocolates sold.

How could rent be a variable cost? If it were a variable cost, how do you think it would affect Sweet Temptations' variable costs line in Exhibit 2-4?

Because graphs are easy to see, we used them to show Sweet Temptations' fixed and variable costs in Exhibits 2-3 and 2-4. For C-V-P analysis, however, it is often better to use equations because they show more precise numbers. For instance, the equation for the total amount of a variable cost is

Total variable cost = vX
where:
v = variable cost per unit sold, and
X = sales volume.

The equation for the variable cost line in Exhibit 2-4 is

Total variable cost of boxes of chocolates sold = $\$4.50X$
where:
X = sales volume.

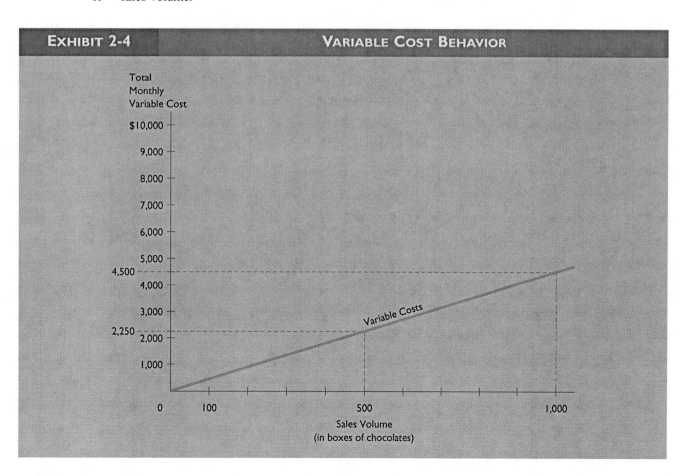

EXHIBIT 2-4   VARIABLE COST BEHAVIOR

Total Costs

Total costs at any volume are the sum of the fixed costs and the variable costs at that volume. For example, at a sales volume of 500 boxes of chocolates, Sweet Temptations' estimated fixed costs are $3,850 and its estimated variable costs are $2,250 (500 × $4.50), for an estimated total cost of $6,100 at that volume. At a sales volume of 1,000 boxes of chocolates, estimated fixed costs are $3,850, estimated variable costs are $4,500 (1,000 × $4.50), and the estimated total cost is $8,350. Exhibit 2-5 illustrates the total cost in relation to sales volume. Notice that if no boxes of chocolates are sold, the total cost will be equal to the fixed costs of $3,850. As sales increase, the total cost will increase by $4.50 per box, the amount of the variable cost per box.

The equation for the total cost is

$$\text{Total cost} = f + vX$$
where:
f = total fixed costs,
v = variable cost per unit sold, and
X = sales volume.

The equation for the total cost line in Exhibit 2-5 is

$$\text{Total cost of boxes of chocolates sold} = \$3{,}850 + \$4.50X$$
where:
X = sales volume.

Now that you understand the relationships of volume, fixed costs, and variable costs to the total cost, we can use C-V-P analysis to estimate profit.

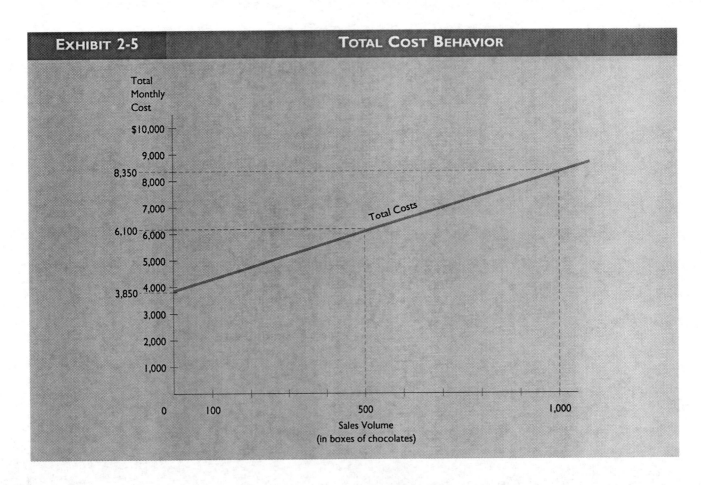

EXHIBIT 2-5   **TOTAL COST BEHAVIOR**

Profit Computation

According to the marketing plan, Sweet Temptations expects to sell 720 boxes of chocolates at $10 each in January. Exhibit 2-6 shows Sweet Temptations' projected income statement in the format that is presented to external users. This is the same format that we discussed in Chapter 1 and illustrated in Exhibit 1-7. External decision makers find this format understandable and use this form of income statement for their investment and credit decisions. This income statement results from the following equation:

$$\text{Net Income (Profit)} = \text{Revenues} - \text{Expenses}$$

In this equation, revenues (the selling prices of all the boxes of chocolates sold to customers) include cash and credit sales, and expenses (the costs of providing the boxes of chocolates to customers) include the cost of boxes of chocolates sold and the expenses to operate the business.

Profit Graph

One way of graphing a company's net income (profit) is to show both its revenues and its costs (expenses) on the same graph. Recall that the graph of a company's total costs includes its fixed costs and its variable costs, as we illustrated in Exhibit 2-5 for Sweet Temptations. The graph of a company's revenues is shown by a straight line sloping upward from the origin of the graph. The slope of the line is the rate (selling price per unit) at which the total revenues increase each time the company sells another unit.

The graph in Exhibit 2-7 shows the estimated total revenue line and the estimated total cost line for Sweet Temptations. Note that the total revenue line crosses the total cost line at 700 boxes of chocolates. At this point, the total revenues will be $7,000, and the total costs will be $7,000, so there will be zero profit. The unit sales volume at which a company earns zero profit is called the **break-even point**. Above the break-even unit sales volume, the total revenues of the company are more than its total costs, so there will be a profit. Below the break-even point, the total revenues are less than the total costs, so there will be a loss. For instance, at a sales volume of 720 boxes of chocolates, the graph in Exhibit 2-7 shows that Sweet Temptations will earn a profit of $110 (as we computed

EXHIBIT 2-6	PROJECTED INCOME STATEMENT FOR EXTERNAL USERS		

SWEET TEMPTATIONS
Projected Income Statement
For the Month Ended January 31, 2011

Revenues:			
Sales revenues			$7,200
Expenses:			
Cost of boxes of chocolates sold		$3,240	
Rent expense		1,000	
Salaries expense		2,050	
Consulting expense		200	
Advertising expense		305	
Supplies expense		30	
Depreciation expense: display cases		15	
Telephone and utilities expense		250	
Total expenses			(7,090)
Net income			$ 110

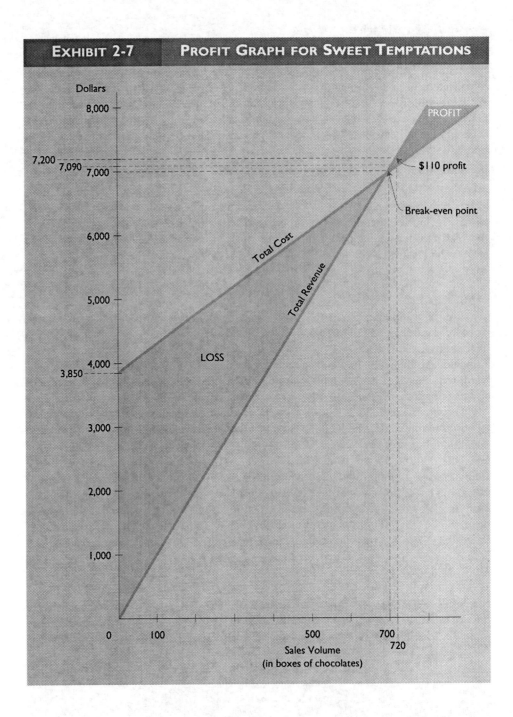

EXHIBIT 2-7   PROFIT GRAPH FOR SWEET TEMPTATIONS

in the income statement in Exhibit 2-6), the difference between the $7,200 estimated total revenue and $7,090 estimated total cost at this volume. Although some decision makers use this type of graph, many others prefer to use a different graph that shows a company's contribution margin, as we discuss next.

Contribution Margin

To estimate profit at different volume levels, the entrepreneur needs C-V-P information in a form that relates the estimated revenues and estimated variable costs to the estimated fixed costs. Exhibit 2-8 shows an income statement containing the same information as Exhibit 2-6, but in a format that is more useful for the internal decision makers in per-

EXHIBIT 2-8	PROJECTED INCOME STATEMENT FOR INTERNAL USERS (CONTRIBUTION MARGIN APPROACH)

SWEET TEMPTATIONS
Projected Income Statement
For the Month Ended January 31, 2011

Total sales revenues ($10 × 720 boxes of chocolates)		$7,200
Less total variable costs:		
Cost of boxes of chocolate sold ($4.50 × 720 boxes)		(3,240)
Total contribution margin		$3,960
Less total fixed costs:		
Rent expense	$1,000	
Salaries expense	2,050	
Consulting expense	200	
Advertising expense	305	
Supplies expense	30	
Depreciation expense: display cases	15	
Telephone and utilities expense	250	
Total fixed costs		(3,850)
Profit		$ 110

forming C-V-P analysis because it shows expenses as variable and fixed. This income statement format is sometimes called the *contribution margin approach.* Notice that, on this income statement, Sweet Temptations first calculates its estimated sales revenue ($7,200) by multiplying the number of boxes of chocolates it expects to sell (720) by the selling price per box ($10). Sweet Temptations next determines the total estimated variable costs of selling the 720 boxes of chocolates ($3,240) by multiplying the number of boxes it expects to sell (720) by the variable cost per box of chocolates ($4.50). These total variable costs are then subtracted from total sales revenue. The $3,960 ($7,200 − $3,240) difference is called the *total contribution margin.*

The **total contribution margin**, at a given sales volume, is the difference between the estimated total sales revenue and the estimated total variable costs. It is the amount of revenue remaining, after subtracting out the total variable costs, that will contribute to "covering" the estimated fixed costs. To compute the estimated profit, we subtract the total estimated fixed costs for the month from the total contribution margin. If the contribution margin is more than the total fixed costs, there will be a profit. If the contribution margin is less than the total fixed costs, there will be a loss. Exhibit 2-8 shows that Sweet Temptations' estimated profit is $110 ($3,960 total contribution margin − $3,850 total fixed costs).

The contribution margin may also be shown on a per-unit basis. The **contribution margin per unit** is the difference between the estimated sales revenue per unit and the estimated variable costs per unit. For Sweet Temptations, the contribution margin per unit is $5.50 ($10 sales revenue − $4.50 variable costs). At 720 units, the total contribution margin will be $3,960 (720 × $5.50), which is the same as shown in Exhibit 2-8. Later, you will see that computing the total contribution margin (by either method described above) is the key to understanding the relationship between profit and sales volume.

Exhibit 2-9 shows what the total contribution margin will be at different unit sales volumes. In this graph, since the contribution margin of one box of chocolates is $5.50, the total contribution margin increases at a rate of $5.50 per box of chocolates sold. For example, at a volume of 500 boxes of chocolates, the contribution margin will be $2,750

| EXHIBIT 2-9 | RELATIONSHIP BETWEEN THE TOTAL CONTRIBUTION MARGIN AND THE UNIT SALES VOLUME |

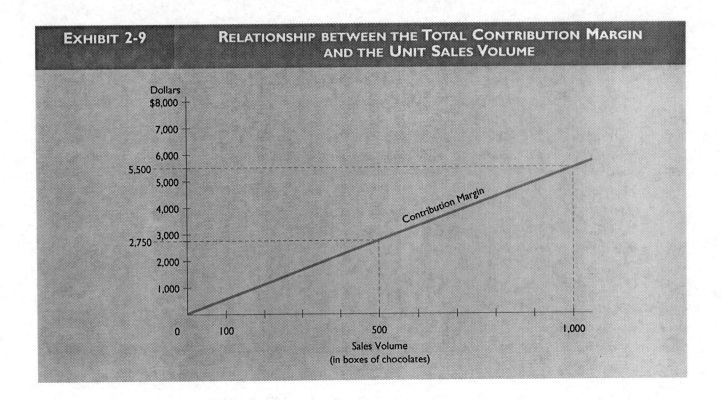

(500 boxes × $5.50). At a volume of 1,000 boxes of chocolates, the contribution margin will be $5,500 (1,000 boxes × $5.50).

 If variable costs were higher per unit, would you expect the contribution margin line in Exhibit 2-9 to be steeper or flatter than it is? Why?

Showing C-V-P Relationships

Now that you understand the contribution margin and fixed costs, we can show the estimated profit or loss at different sales volumes in a graph. Exhibit 2-10 shows how sales volume affects the estimated profit (or loss) for Sweet Temptations. Two lines are drawn on this graph. One line shows the estimated total contribution margin at different sales volumes. It is the same line as shown in Exhibit 2-9. The other line shows the $3,850 total estimated fixed costs. The vertical distance between these lines is the estimated profit or loss at the different sales volumes. Remember, estimated profit is the total contribution margin minus the estimated total fixed costs. Note that this graph shows that Sweet Temptations will earn $0 profit if it sells 700 boxes of chocolates; this is its break-even point. Above the break-even unit sales volume (such as at a volume of 1,000 boxes), the total contribution margin ($5,500) is more than the total estimated fixed costs ($3,850), so there would be a profit ($5,500 − $3,850 = $1,650). Below the break-even point (such as at a volume of 500 boxes), the total contribution margin ($2,750) is less than the total estimated fixed costs, so there would be a loss ($2,750 − $3,850 = −$1,100).

 If fixed costs were greater, would you expect Sweet Temptations to break even at a lower sales volume or a higher sales volume? Why?

Profit Computation (Equation Form)

In Exhibit 2-10, we show a graph of the C-V-P relationships for Sweet Temptations. Graphs are usually a helpful tool for an entrepreneur (and students!) to see a "picture" of these relationships. Sometimes, however, an entrepreneur (or student) does not need a pic-

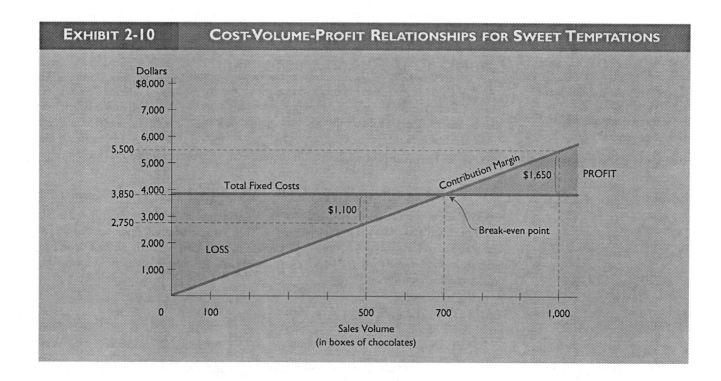

EXHIBIT 2-10   COST-VOLUME-PROFIT RELATIONSHIPS FOR SWEET TEMPTATIONS

ture to understand the relationships. In this case, using equations may be a better and faster way to understand C-V-P relationships. (You may have already thought of these equations as you studied Exhibit 2-10.) In this section, we look at how to use equations for C-V-P analysis to answer the following questions:

1. How much profit will the company earn at a given unit sales volume?
2. How many units must the company sell to break even?
3. How many units must the company sell to earn a given amount of profit? (The given amount is usually a desired profit that the company uses as a goal.)

In the following discussion, we use Sweet Temptations' revenue and cost information from the projected income statement for internal decision makers, in Exhibit 2-8. We determined the total sales revenue by multiplying the selling price per unit by the estimated sales volume. We determined the total estimated variable costs by multiplying the variable cost per unit by the same sales volume. And we subtracted the total estimated variable and fixed costs from the total estimated sales revenue to determine the estimated profit. We can show this in a "profit equation" as follows:

$$\text{Profit (for a given sales volume)} = \left[\begin{array}{ccc}\text{Selling price per unit} & \times & \text{Unit sales volume}\end{array}\right] - \left[\begin{array}{ccc}\text{Variable cost per unit} & \times & \text{Unit sales volume}\end{array}\right] - \begin{array}{c}\text{Total fixed costs}\end{array}$$

The profit equation can be used in C-V-P analysis. For Sweet Temptations, for instance, if we use X to stand for a given sales volume of boxes of chocolates, and if we include the estimated selling price and variable cost per unit, the equation is written as follows:

$$\text{Profit} = \$10X - \$4.50X - \$3,850$$
$$= (\$10 - \$4.50)X - \$3,850$$
$$= \$5.50X - \$3,850$$

This equation, then, can be used in solving various C-V-P questions for Sweet Temptations.[4]

USING C-V-P ANALYSIS

C-V-P analysis is useful in planning because it shows the impact of alternative plans on profit. This analysis can help the entrepreneur make planning decisions and can help investors and creditors evaluate the risk associated with their investment and credit decisions. For instance, suppose Anna has asked you to answer, for Sweet Temptations, the three questions we mentioned earlier. In this section we describe how to do so.

Estimating Profit at Given Unit Sales Volume

Suppose Anna wants you to estimate Sweet Temptations' monthly profit if it sells 750 boxes of chocolates (i.e., a unit sales volume of 750 boxes) a month. Remember that Sweet Temptations' selling price is $10 per unit and its variable cost is $4.50 per unit. You can estimate monthly profit when 750 boxes of chocolates are sold in a month by using the profit equation as follows:

$$\text{Profit} = \left[\begin{array}{c}\text{Selling} \\ \text{price} \\ \text{per unit}\end{array} \times \begin{array}{c}\text{Unit} \\ \text{sales} \\ \text{volume}\end{array}\right] - \left[\begin{array}{c}\text{Variable} \\ \text{cost} \\ \text{per unit}\end{array} \times \begin{array}{c}\text{Unit} \\ \text{sales} \\ \text{volume}\end{array}\right] - \begin{array}{c}\text{Total} \\ \text{fixed} \\ \text{costs}\end{array}$$

$$= (\$10 \times 750) - (\$4.50 \times 750) - \$3,850$$
$$= \$7,500 - \$3,375 - \$3,850$$
$$= \underline{\$275}$$

Thus, you can tell Anna that Sweet Temptations will make a monthly profit of $275 if it sells 750 boxes of chocolates a month.

Finding the Break-Even Point

Suppose Anna wants you to estimate how many boxes of chocolates Sweet Temptations must sell to break even each month. Recall that the break-even point is the unit sales volume that results in zero profit. This occurs when total sales revenue equals total costs (total variable costs plus total fixed costs). To find the break-even point, we start with the profit equation. Remember that the contribution margin per unit is the difference between the sales revenue per unit and the variable costs per unit. With this in mind, we can rearrange the profit equation[5] into a break-even equation as follows:

---

[4]Note in the last line of the equation that the $5.50 is the contribution margin per unit. This can come in handy as a "shortcut" when using the profit equation, so that the equation becomes:

$$\begin{array}{c}\text{Profit} \\ \text{(for a given} \\ \text{sales volume)}\end{array} = \left[\begin{array}{c}\text{Contribution} \\ \text{margin} \\ \text{per unit}\end{array} \times \begin{array}{c}\text{Unit} \\ \text{sales} \\ \text{volume}\end{array}\right] - \begin{array}{c}\text{Total} \\ \text{fixed} \\ \text{costs}\end{array}$$

[5]For those of you who want "proof" of this break-even equation, since the contribution margin per unit is the selling price per unit minus the variable cost per unit, we can substitute the total contribution margin per unit into the profit equation as follows:

$$\text{Profit} = \left[\begin{array}{c}\text{Contribution} \\ \text{margin} \\ \text{per unit}\end{array} \times \begin{array}{c}\text{Unit} \\ \text{sales} \\ \text{volume}\end{array}\right] - \begin{array}{c}\text{Total} \\ \text{fixed} \\ \text{costs}\end{array}$$

Since break-even occurs when profit is zero, we can omit the profit, move the total fixed costs to the other side of the equation, and rewrite the equation as follows:

$$\text{Total fixed costs} = \left[\begin{array}{c}\text{Contribution} \\ \text{margin} \\ \text{per unit}\end{array} \times \begin{array}{c}\text{Unit} \\ \text{sales} \\ \text{volume}\end{array}\right]$$

Finally, we can divide both sides of the equation by the contribution margin per unit to derive the break-even equation:

$$\frac{\text{Total fixed costs}}{\text{Contribution margin per unit}} = \begin{array}{c}\text{Unit sales volume} \\ \text{(to earn zero profit)}\end{array}$$

---

4 What must decision makers be able to predict in order to estimate profit at a given sales volume?

5 How can decision makers predict the sales volume necessary for estimated revenues to cover estimated costs?

$$\frac{\text{Unit sales volume}}{\text{(to earn zero profit)}} = \frac{\text{Total fixed costs}}{\text{Contribution margin per unit}}$$

So for Sweet Temptations, you can tell Anna that the break-even point is 700 boxes of chocolates, computed using the break-even equation as follows (letting X stand for the unit sales volume):

$$\frac{\text{Unit sales volume}}{\text{(to earn zero profit)}} = \frac{\$3,850 \text{ total fixed costs}}{(\$10 \text{ selling price} - \$4.50 \text{ variable cost}) \text{ per unit}}$$

$$X = \frac{\$3,850}{\$5.50}$$

$$X = \underline{700} \text{ boxes of chocolates}$$

You can verify the break-even sales volume of 700 boxes of chocolates with the following schedule:

Total sales revenue (700 boxes of chocolates @ $10.00 per box)	$7,000
Less: Total variable costs (700 boxes of chocolates @ $4.50 per box)	(3,150)
Total contribution margin (700 boxes of chocolates @ $5.50 per box)	$3,850
Less: Total fixed costs	(3,850)
Profit	$ 0

Finding the Unit Sales Volume to Achieve a Target Profit

Finding the break-even point gives the entrepreneur useful information. However, most entrepreneurs are interested in earning a profit that is high enough to satisfy their goals and the company's goals. A company often states its profit goals at amounts that result in a satisfactory return on the average total assets used in its operations. Since this is an introduction to C-V-P analysis, we will wait to discuss what is meant by "satisfactory return" and "average total assets" until Chapter 10. Here we will assume an amount of profit that is satisfactory. Suppose Anna's goal is that Sweet Temptations earn a profit of $110 per month. How many boxes of chocolates must Sweet Temptations sell per month to earn $110 profit? To answer this question, we slightly modify the break-even equation.

6 How can decision makers predict the sales volume necessary to achieve a target profit?

The break-even point is the sales volume at which the total contribution margin is equal to, or "covers," the total fixed costs. Therefore, each additional unit sold above the break-even sales volume increases profit by the contribution margin per unit. Hence, to find the sales volume at which the total contribution margin "covers" both total fixed costs *and* the desired profit, we can modify the break-even equation simply by adding the desired profit to fixed costs, as follows:

$$\frac{\text{Unit sales volume}}{\text{(to earn desired profit)}} = \frac{\text{Total fixed costs} + \text{Desired profit}}{\text{Contribution margin per unit}}$$

So, if we let X stand for the unit sales volume, Sweet Temptations needs to sell 720 boxes of chocolates to earn a profit of $110 a month, computed as follows:

$$X = \frac{\$3,850 + \$110}{\$5.50 \text{ per box of chocolates}}$$

$$X = \underline{720} \text{ boxes of chocolates}$$

You can verify the $110 profit with the following schedule.

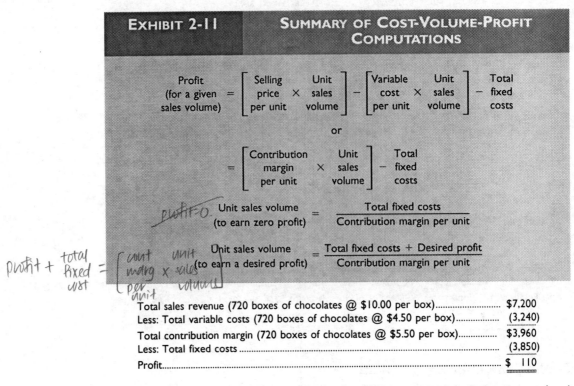

EXHIBIT 2-11	SUMMARY OF COST-VOLUME-PROFIT COMPUTATIONS

$$\text{Profit (for a given sales volume)} = \left[\text{Selling price per unit} \times \text{Unit sales volume}\right] - \left[\text{Variable cost per unit} \times \text{Unit sales volume}\right] - \text{Total fixed costs}$$

or

$$= \left[\text{Contribution margin per unit} \times \text{Unit sales volume}\right] - \text{Total fixed costs}$$

profit = 0

$$\text{Unit sales volume (to earn zero profit)} = \frac{\text{Total fixed costs}}{\text{Contribution margin per unit}}$$

$$\text{Unit sales volume (to earn a desired profit)} = \frac{\text{Total fixed costs} + \text{Desired profit}}{\text{Contribution margin per unit}}$$

[handwritten: profit + total fixed cost = [cont marg per unit × unit sales volume]]

Total sales revenue (720 boxes of chocolates @ $10.00 per box).......................... $7,200
Less: Total variable costs (720 boxes of chocolates @ $4.50 per box)................. (3,240)
Total contribution margin (720 boxes of chocolates @ $5.50 per box)............... $3,960
Less: Total fixed costs .... (3,850)
Profit.. $ 110

Since Anna had included the desired profit of $110 per month in Sweet Temptations' business plan, the income statement for internal decision makers shown in Exhibit 2-8 is an expanded version of the preceding schedule.

Summary of the C-V-P Analysis Computations

Exhibit 2-11 summarizes the equations that we used in our discussion of C-V-P analysis. Although it may be tempting to try to memorize them, you should strive to understand how these equations relate to one another.

OTHER PLANNING ISSUES

7 How can decision makers use accounting information to evaluate alternative plans?

Providing answers to the previous three questions showed how C-V-P analysis is useful in planning. There are many other planning issues for which C-V-P analysis provides useful information. For instance, suppose you and Anna are considering alternative plans for Sweet Temptations to raise its monthly profit. These plans include:

1. Raising the selling price of the boxes of chocolates to $11 per box. With this alternative, the variable costs per box of chocolates and the total fixed costs do not change.

2. Purchasing a premium line of chocolates rather than the superior line, thus increasing the variable costs to $4.60 per box. You and Anna are considering this alternative because the improvement in the quality of the chocolate may cause the sales volume of boxes of chocolates to increase. With this change, neither the selling price per unit nor the total fixed costs change.

3. Increasing the total fixed costs by spending $110 more on advertising. With this alternative, the selling price per unit and the variable costs per unit do not change, but the additional advertising may cause an increase in sales volume.

How would you modify the graph in Exhibit 2-10 to provide information for Plan #1?

We do not show C-V-P analysis for these three issues at this time because we will discuss similar issues in Chapter 10. We raise these issues here to get you to think about how to use the C-V-P equations or graphs to provide helpful information. The C-V-P analysis for these three alternative plans, however, does not provide all the information you need to make a decision. It is a helpful tool, but it is most effective when used with critical thinking. You must think about the effects each of the alternatives has on your customers.

For instance, each of the alternatives is likely to affect the number of boxes of chocolates that Sweet Temptations can sell. A change in selling price would certainly affect your customers' decisions to purchase boxes of chocolates. A decrease in selling price would bring the boxes of chocolates into the spending range of more people (probably increasing the number of boxes of chocolates you could sell), whereas an increase in selling price may make the boxes of chocolates too expensive for some customers (possibly decreasing the number of boxes of chocolates you could sell). Selling a higher quality of chocolates may attract a different, or additional, group of customers, thus affecting sales volume. Increasing advertising may make more people aware of, and may attract more customers to, Sweet Temptations. Before you make a decision, you should consider how it will affect customers' interest in your product and estimate the probable unit sales volume for each alternative. Then, for whatever sales volume you expect, the analysis can provide a more realistic profit estimate.

WHAT CAN HAPPEN IF A COMPANY DOESN'T HAVE A BUSINESS PLAN[b]

As the last century ended, many Internet companies were in such a rush to join their apparently wildly successful dot-com peers that they forgot one small detail: a sound business plan. Here is a history lesson. By the end of 2001, more than 519 dot-com companies had failed. Some went bankrupt; others had to make radical adjustments to the way they conducted business, including massive layoffs (98,522 employees in one year). Some such as Art.com and Wine.com began again with new owners and business plans, and still others simply shut down their Web sites.

A look back on that period reveals that many of those companies needed huge revenue growths just to break even. For example, the revenue of Tickets.com had increased by 38.77% during one year—but in order to break even, the company's revenue would have had to grow 606.7%! Nineteen companies had an even more grim situation. The worst was E-Loan, whose revenue had increased by 85.24% during the same year—but whose revenue would have had to grow 5,065.2% in order for the company to break even! Both of these companies had failed by the end of the year.

What happened? Many company owners, in an effort to compete and attract customers, thought they could start out selling their products for less than what they paid for them and then, after increasing their volume of customers, make up the difference later by raising the selling prices of their products. This means that they started out with negative contribution margins, causing them to lose money right from the start on every sale that they made. (And for some companies, even the low selling prices didn't attract enough customers.) Unfortunately, there was no "later," because these companies ran out of capital or attracted an insufficient number of customers to "make a go of it." Additionally, some owners didn't consider the extremely high costs necessary to run and advertise a Web site (particularly the marketing and salary costs), as well as the costs of storing and distributing their companies' products.

A business plan, along with its C-V-P analysis, could have helped the owners of these companies discover the "flaws" in their thinking before their companies got into trouble. With C-V-P analysis it would have been easy for them to confirm that the planned selling prices of their products initially would not have been high enough, *at any volume,* for the companies to break even. Furthermore, a business plan would have focused the owners' attention on the high marketing and salary costs, and the product storage and distribution costs, thereby helping the owners determine the selling prices that would most likely help their companies break even *and* earn desired profits. A business plan also could have helped the owners see the possible effects on their companies' profits of sales predictions that were too optimistic or too pessimistic.

BUSINESS ISSUES AND VALUES: WASTE NOT, WANT NOT

C-V-P accounting information is one factor that influences business decisions, but entrepreneurs also need to consider the nonfinancial effects of their decisions. For example, if the managers of a company are thinking about lowering the company's total costs by omitting toxic waste cleanup around the factory, they must ask questions such as the following: What will be the impact on the environment? What health effects might the employees suffer later? What might be the health impact on the company's neighbors? Legally, can we even consider not cleaning up the toxic waste? Although omitting toxic waste cleanup may reduce total costs dramatically, these managers might consider the other, more-difficult-to-measure costs to be too high. Therefore, after weighing all the factors surrounding the alternatives, the managers may choose a more socially acceptable alternative that results in a less favorable profit.

SUMMARY

At the beginning of the chapter we asked you several questions. During the chapter, we asked you to STOP and answer some additional questions to build your knowledge about specific issues. Be sure you answered these additional questions. Below are the questions from the beginning of the chapter, with a brief summary of the key points relating to the answers. Use your creative and critical thinking skills to expand on these key points to develop more complete answers to the questions and to determine what other questions you have that might lead you to learn more about the issues.

1 Since the future is uncertain and circumstances are likely to change, why should a company bother to plan?

A business plan helps the owners or managers of a company organize the company, serves as a benchmark against which they can evaluate actual company performance, and helps the company obtain financing. The business plan consists of a description of the company, a marketing plan, an operating plan, and a financial plan. Accounting information contributes to the planning process by providing information for C-V-P analysis and by including in the financial plan the effects that estimated revenues, variable costs, and fixed costs have on the company's profits.

2 What should a company include in its business plan?

A business plan should include a description of the company, a marketing plan, an operating plan, and a financial plan. The description should include information about the organization of the company, its products or services, its current and potential customers, its objectives, where it is located, and where it conducts business. The marketing plan shows how the company will make sales and how it will influence and respond to market conditions. The operating plan includes a description of the relationships between the company, its suppliers, and its customers, as well as a description of how the company will develop, service, protect, and support its products or services. The financial plan identifies the company's capital requirements and sources of capital, and describes the company's projected financial performance.

3 How does accounting information contribute to the planning process?

Accountants determine how revenues, variable costs, and fixed costs affect profits based on their observations of how costs "behave" and on their estimates of future revenues and costs. By observing cost behavior patterns, accountants are able to classify the costs as fixed or variable, and then to use this classification to predict the amounts of the costs at different activity levels. Accounting information, then, can help decision-makers evaluate alternative plans by using C-V-P analysis to show the profit effect of each plan. C-V-P analysis is a tool that helps managers think critically about the different aspects of each plan.

4 **What must decision makers be able to predict in order to estimate profit at a given sales volume?**

To estimate profit at a given sales volume, decision makers must be able to predict the product's selling price, the costs that the company will incur, and the behavior of those costs (whether they are fixed or variable costs). The fixed costs will not change because of sales volume, but the variable costs will change directly with changes in sales volume.

5 **How can decision makers predict the sales volume necessary for estimated revenues to cover estimated costs?**

To predict the sales volume necessary for estimated revenues to cover estimated costs, decision makers must rearrange the profit equation into the break-even equation. Using what they know about the product's selling price and the behavior of the company's costs, the decision makers can determine the contribution margin per unit of product by subtracting the estimated variable costs per unit from the product's estimated selling price. Then they can substitute the contribution margin and the estimated fixed costs into the equation and solve for the necessary sales volume.

6 **How can decision makers predict the sales volume necessary to achieve a target profit?**

Predicting the sales volume necessary to achieve a target profit is not very different from predicting the sales volume necessary for estimated revenues to cover estimated costs. The only difference is that the decision makers must modify the break-even equation by adding the desired profit to the estimated fixed costs. Then, after substituting the contribution margin and the estimated fixed costs plus the desired profit into the equation, they can solve for the necessary sales volume.

7 **How can decision makers use accounting information to evaluate alternative plans?**

Decision makers can determine how changes in costs and revenues affect the company's profit. Based on accounting information alone, the alternative that leads to the highest profit will be the best solution. However, decision makers should also consider the nonfinancial effects that their decisions may have.

KEY TERMS

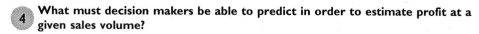

break-even point *(p. 53)*
business plan *(p. 41)*
capital *(p. 45)*
contribution margin per unit *(p. 55)*
cost-volume-profit (**C-V-P**) analysis
    (p. 48)
fixed costs *(p. 49)*
line of credit *(p. 46)*

long-term capital *(p. 47)*
return *(p. 41)*
risk *(p. 41)*
short-term capital *(p. 46)*
total contribution margin *(p. 55)*
total costs *(p. 52)*
variable cost *(p. 50)*
volume *(p. 48)*

SUMMARY SURFING

Here is an opportunity to gather information on the Internet about real-world issues related to the topics in this chapter (for suggestions on how to navigate various organizations' Web sites to find the relevant information, see the related discussion in the Preface at the beginning of the book). Answer the following questions.

- Go to the **SBA** (**U.S. Small Business Administration**) Web site. What are the three elements of a business plan? Identify a few components under each section. What are the four distinct sections of a business plan? How do these compare with what we discussed in the chapter?

- Go to the **SBA** (**U.S. Small Business Administration**) Web site. In the examples of real business plans, find an industry in which you are interested, locate a company within that industry and review that company's business plan. What is the company's market? What does the company estimate that its sales must be in order to break even?

INTEGRATED BUSINESS AND ACCOUNTING SITUATIONS

Answer the Following Questions in Your Own Words.

Testing Your Knowledge

2-1 Since the future is uncertain and circumstances are likely to change, why should the managers and owners of a company bother to plan?

2-2 Describe the three main functions of a business plan.

2-3 Describe the components of a business plan. How does each of these components help an investor, a creditor, and a manager or owner make decisions about a company?

2-4 Why is it important for a company to have a cash buffer on hand?

2-5 How can an entrepreneur determine a company's capital requirements?

2-6 What is the difference between short-term and long-term capital?

2-7 Explain what cost-volume-profit analysis is.

2-8 How does cost-volume-profit analysis help entrepreneurs develop their companies' business plans?

2-9 How can you tell whether a cost is a variable cost or a fixed cost?

2-10 What is a contribution margin?

2-11 Explain what it means when a company breaks even.

2-12 Indicate the effect (increase, decrease, no change, or not enough information) that each of the following situations has on break-even unit sales. If you answer "not enough information," list the information that you need in order to be able to determine the effect.
   (a) A retail company purchases price tags to use in place of the stickers it has used in the past.
   (b) An athletic equipment store leases more retail space.
   (c) A bakery increases its advertising expense.

(d) A merchandiser plans to increase the selling price of its product. To counter potential decreases in sales, the merchandiser also plans to increase the amount of per-product commission that the sales staff earns.

(e) An accounting firm plans to increase its billing rate per hour.

(f) A retail company has found a supplier that will provide the same merchandise its old supplier provided, but at a lower price.

(g) A private college in the Northwest installs air conditioning in its dormitories.

(h) A retail company reduces advertising expenses and increases the commissions of its sales force.

(i) Instead of having its office building cleaned by a cleaning service, a company plans to hire its own cleaning crew.

2-13 If the total variable cost per unit increases while the selling price per unit, the fixed costs, and the sales volume remain the same, how would you expect the change in variable costs to affect profit? the break-even point?

2-14 If total fixed costs increase while the selling price per unit, the variable costs per unit, and the sales volume remain the same, how would you expect the change in fixed costs to affect profit? the break-even point?

2-15 How does the income statement shown in Exhibit 2-8 help internal decision makers perform cost-volume-profit analysis?

Applying Your Knowledge

2-16 Imagine that you are going to start your own company. Think about the concept for a minute.

Required: What will you call your company? What kind of product or service will you sell? What price will you charge for your product or service? Why? What variable costs and what fixed costs do you think you will incur?

2-17 Suppose you want to start a company that sells sports equipment.

Required: Go to the reference section of your library. What type of information can you find in *Moody's* or *Standard & Poor's* to help you prepare projected financial statements for your company?

2-18 TLC Company sells a single product, a food basket (containing fruit, cheese, nuts, and other items) that friends and family can purchase for college students who need a little extra TLC. This product, called the Exam-O-Rama, sells for $10 per basket. The variable cost is $6 per basket, and the total fixed cost is $24,000 per year.

Required: (1) Draw one graph showing TLC's (a) total revenues and (b) total costs as volume varies. Locate the break-even point on the graph.
(2) What is TLC's profit equation in terms of units sold?
(3) What is TLC's break-even point in units?

2-19 Bathtub Rings Company sells shower-curtain rings for $1.60 per box. The variable cost is $1.20 per box, and the fixed cost totals $20,000 per year.

Required: (1) What is Bathtub Rings' profit equation in terms of boxes of shower-curtain rings sold?
(2) Draw a graph of Bathtub Rings' total contribution margin and total fixed cost as volume varies. Locate the break-even point on this graph.
(3) What is Bathtub Rings' break-even point in units?
(4) What would total profits be if Bathtub Rings sold 500,000 boxes of shower-curtain rings?
(5) How many boxes of shower-curtain rings would Bathtub Rings have to sell to earn $50,000 of profit?

2-20 Go Figure Company sells small calculators for $12 each. This year, Go Figure's fixed cost totals $110,000. The variable cost per calculator is $7.

Required: (1) Compute the break-even point in number of calculators.

(2) Compute the number of calculators required to earn a profit of $70,000.

(3) If the total fixed cost increases to $160,000 next year,

    (a) what will Go Figure's break-even point be in number of calculators?

    (b) what profit (or loss) will Go Figure have if it sells 30,000 calculators?

    (c) how many calculators will Go Figure have to sell to earn a profit of $70,000?

2-21 Silencer Company sells a single product, mufflers for leaf blowers. The company's profit computation for last year is shown here:

Sales revenue (2,000 units @ $25)	$50,000
Less variable costs	(20,000)
Contribution margin	$30,000
Less fixed costs	(22,000)
Profit	$ 8,000

Silencer has decided to increase the price of its product to $30 per muffler. The company believes that if it increases its fixed advertising (selling) cost by $3,400, sales volume next year will be 1,800 mufflers. Variable cost per muffler will be unchanged.

Required: (1) Using the above income statement format, show the computation of expected profit for Silencer's operations next year.

(2) How many mufflers would Silencer have to sell to earn as much profit next year as it did last year?

(3) Do you agree with Silencer's decision? Explain why or why not.

2-22 Rapunzel Company currently sells a single product, shampoo, for $4 per bottle. The variable cost per bottle is $3. Rapunzel's fixed cost totals $6,000.

Required: (1) Compute the following amounts for Rapunzel Company:

    (a) Contribution margin per bottle of shampoo

    (b) Break-even point in bottles of shampoo

    (c) The profit that Rapunzel will earn at a sales volume of 25,000 bottles of shampoo

    (d) The number of bottles of shampoo that Rapunzel must sell to earn a profit of $16,000

(2) Rapunzel is considering increasing its total fixed cost to $8,000 and then also increasing the selling price of its product to $5. The variable cost per bottle of shampoo would remain unchanged. Repeat the computations from (1), using this new information. Will this decision be a good one for Rapunzel? Why or why not?

(3) Draw a graph with four lines to show the following:

    (a) Total contribution margin earned when Rapunzel sells from 0 to 10,000 bottles of shampoo at a selling price of $4 per bottle

    (b) Total contribution margin earned when Rapunzel sells from 0 to 10,000 bottles of shampoo at a selling price of $5 per bottle

    (c) Rapunzel's fixed cost total of $6,000

    (d) Rapunzel's fixed cost total of $8,000

    (e) Rapunzel's break-even point in bottles of shampoo before and after the selling price and fixed cost changes

(4) Does the graph support your conclusion in (2) above? If so, how does it support your conclusion? If not, what new or different information did you get from the graph?

2-23 The Body Shop Equipment Company sells a small, relatively lightweight multipurpose exercise machine. This machine sells for $700. A recent cost analysis shows that The Body Shop's cost structure for the coming year is as follows:

Variable cost per unit	$ 325
Total annual fixed costs	125,000

Required: (1) Draw a graph that clearly shows (a) total fixed cost, (b) total cost, (c) total sales revenue, and (d) total contribution margin as the sales volume of exercise machines increases. Locate the break-even point on the graph.

(2) Compute the break-even point in number of machines.

(3) How many machines must the Body Shop sell to earn $30,000 of profit per year?

(4) How much profit would be earned at a sales volume of $420,000?

(5) Sean McLean, the owner of the Body Shop Equipment Company, is considering traveling a circuit of gyms and fitness centers around the United States each year to demonstrate the exercise machine, distribute information, and obtain sales contracts. He estimates that this will cost about $6,000 per year. How many additional exercise machines must the company sell per year to cover the cost of this effort?

2-24 Lady MacBeth Company sells bottles of dry cleaning solvent (spot remover) for $10 each. The variable cost for each bottle is $4. Lady MacBeth's total fixed cost for the year is $3,600.

Required: (1) Answer the following questions about the company's break-even point.

(a) How many bottles of spot remover must Lady MacBeth sell to break even?

(b) How would your answer to (1a) change if Lady MacBeth lowered the selling price per bottle by $2? What if, instead, it raised the selling price by $2?

(c) How would your answer to (1a) change if Lady MacBeth raised the variable cost per bottle by $2? What if, instead, it lowered the variable cost by $2?

(d) How would your answer to (1a) change if Lady MacBeth increased the total fixed cost by $60? What if, instead, Lady MacBeth decreased the total fixed cost by $60?

(2) Answer the following questions about the company's profit.

(a) How many bottles must Lady MacBeth sell to earn $4,800 profit?

(b) How would your answer to (2a) change if Lady MacBeth lowered the selling price per bottle by $2?

(c) Suppose that for every $1 the selling price per bottle decreases below its current selling price of $10 per bottle, Lady MacBeth predicts sales volume will increase by 325 bottles. Assume that before lowering the selling price, Lady MacBeth predicts that it can sell exactly 1,400 bottles. Can Lady MacBeth earn $4,800 profit by lowering the selling price per bottle by $2? Explain why or why not.

(d) Suppose that for every $1 the selling price per bottle increases above its current selling price of $10 per bottle, Lady MacBeth predicts sales volume will decrease by 200 bottles. Assume that before raising the selling price, Lady MacBeth predicts that it can sell exactly 1,400 bottles. Can Lady MacBeth earn $4,800 profit by raising the selling price per bottle by $2? Explain why or why not.

(e) How would your answer to (2a) change if Lady MacBeth raised the variable cost per bottle by $2? What if, instead, it lowered the variable cost per bottle by $2?

(f) How would your answer to (2a) change if Lady MacBeth raised the total fixed cost by $60? What if, instead, Lady MacBeth lowered the total fixed cost by $60?

2-25 The Brickhouse Company is planning to lease a fuel-efficient, hybrid delivery van for its northern sales territory. The leasing company is willing to lease the van under three alternative plans:

Plan A—Brickhouse would pay $0.34 per mile and buy its own gas.
Plan B—Brickhouse would pay $320 per month plus $0.10 per mile and buy its own gas.
Plan C—Brickhouse would pay $960 per month, and the leasing company would pay for all gas.

The leasing company will pay for all repairs and maintenance, insurance, license fees, and so on. Gas should cost $0.06 per mile.

Required: Using miles driven as the units of volume, do the following:
- (1) Write out the cost equation for the cost of operating the delivery van under each of the three plans.
- (2) Graph the three cost equations on the same graph (put cost on the vertical axis and miles driven per month on the horizontal axis).
- (3) Determine at what mileage per month the cost of Plan A would equal the cost of Plan B.
- (4) Determine at what mileage per month the cost of Plan B would equal the cost of Plan C.
- (5) Compute the cost, under each of the three plans, of driving 3,500 miles per month.

2-26   The Mallory Motors Company sells small electric motors for $2 per motor. Variable costs are $1.20 per unit, and fixed costs total $60,000 per year.

Required: (1) Write out Mallory's profit equation in terms of motors sold.
- (2) Draw a graph of Mallory's total contribution margin and total fixed cost as volume varies. Locate the break-even point on this graph.
- (3) Compute Mallory's break-even point in units.
- (4) What total profit would Mallory expect if it sold 500,000 motors?
- (5) How many motors would Mallory have to sell to earn $40,000 profit?

2-27   The Campcraft Company is a small manufacturer of camping trailers. The company manufactures only one model and sells the units for $2,500 each. The variable costs of manufacturing and selling each trailer are $1,900. The total fixed cost amounts to $180,000 per year.

Required: (1) Compute Campcraft's contribution margin per trailer.
- (2) Compute Campcraft's profit (or loss) at a sales volume of 160 trailers.
- (3) Compute the number of units that Campcraft must sell for it to break even.
- (4) Compute the number of units that Campcraft must sell for it to earn a profit of $30,000.

2-28   This year Babco's fixed costs total $110,000. The company sells babushkas for $13 each. The variable cost per babushka is $8.

Required: (1) Compute the break-even point in number of babushkas.
- (2) Compute the number of babushkas that Babco must sell to earn a profit of $70,000.
- (3) If the total fixed cost increases to $150,000 next year,
  - (a) what will be Babco's break-even point in babushkas?
  - (b) what profit (or loss) will Babco have if it sells 28,000 babushkas?
  - (c) how many babushkas will Babco have to sell to earn a profit of $70,000?

2-29   The Cardiff Company sells a single product for $40 per unit. Its total fixed cost amounts to $360,000 per year, and its variable cost per unit is $34.

Required: (1) Compute the following amounts for the Cardiff Company:
- (a) Contribution margin per unit
- (b) Break-even point in units
- (c) The number of units that must be sold to earn $30,000 profit
- (2) Repeat all computations in (1), assuming Cardiff decides to increase its selling price per unit to $44. Assume that the total fixed cost and the variable cost per unit remain the same.

Making Evaluations

2-30   Suppose your wealthy Aunt Gert gave you and your cousins $10,000 each. Assume for a moment that you are not associated with Sweet Temptations and that you are considering loaning the $10,000 to Sweet Temptations.

Required: From the information included in Sweet Temptations' business plan so far, do you think this would be a wise investment on your part? Why or why not? What else would you like to know before making a decision (you don't have to limit your thinking to Sweet Temptations)?

2-31 Refer to 2-30. What if Aunt Gert instead gave you $100,000 and you were interested in investing it in Sweet Temptations?

Required: Would this change your answers to 2-30? Why or why not?

2-32 Joe Billy Ray Bob's Country and Western Company sells a single product—cowboy hats—for $24 per hat. The total fixed cost is $180,000 per year, and the variable cost per hat is $15.

Required: (1) Compute the following amounts for Joe Billy Ray Bob's Country and Western Company:
- (a) Contribution margin per hat
- (b) Break-even point in hats
- (c) The numbers of hats that must be sold to earn $27,000 of profit

(2) Repeat all computations in (1), assuming Joe Billy Ray Bob's decides to increase its selling price per hat to $25. Assume that the total fixed cost and the variable cost per hat remain the same.

(3) Do you agree with Joe Billy Ray Bob's decision to increase its selling price per hat? What other factors should the managers consider in making this decision?

2-33 The Vend-O-Bait Company operates and services bait vending machines placed in gas stations, motels, and restaurants surrounding a large lake. Vend-O-Bait rents 200 machines from the manufacturer. It also rents the space occupied by the machines at each location where it places the machines. Arnie Bass, the company's owner, has two employees who service the machines. Monthly fixed costs for the company are as follows:

Machine rental:	
200 machines × $100 per month.................................	$20,000
Space rental:	
200 locations × $60 per month....................................	12,000
Employee wages:	
2 employees × $800 per month.................................	1,600
Other fixed costs..	2,400
Total	$36,000

Currently, Vend-O-Bait's only variable costs are the costs of the night crawlers, which it purchases for $1.20 per pack. Vend-O-Bait sells these night crawlers for $1.80 per pack.

Required: (1) Answer the following questions:
- (a) What is the monthly break-even point (in packs sold)?
- (b) Compute Vend-O-Bait's monthly profit at monthly sales volumes of 52,000, 56,000, 64,000, and 68,000 packs, respectively.

(2) Suppose that instead of paying $60 fixed rent per month, Arnie Bass could arrange to pay $0.20 for each pack of night crawlers sold at each location to rent the space occupied by the machines. Repeat all computations in (1).

(3) Would it be desirable for Arnie Bass to try to change his space rental from a fixed cost ($60 per location) to a variable cost ($0.20 per pack sold)? Why or why not?

2-34 Refer to 2-24. Suppose your boss at Lady MacBeth is considering some alternative plans and would like your input on the following three independent alternatives:
- (a) Increase the selling price per bottle by $3
- (b) Decrease the variable cost per bottle by $2 by purchasing an equally effective, but less "environmentally friendly," solvent from your supplier
- (c) Decrease the total fixed cost by $1,260.

Assume again that Lady MacBeth currently sells bottles of dry cleaning solvent for $10 each, the variable cost for each bottle is $4, and the total fixed cost for the year is $3,600.

Required: (1) How many bottles would Lady MacBeth have to sell to break even under each of the alternatives? Using this accounting information alone, write your boss a memo in which you recommend an alternative.

(2) Maybe your boss would like to earn a profit of $4,320. How many bottles would Lady MacBeth have to sell to earn a profit of $4,320 under each of the alternatives? Which of the three alternatives would you recommend to your boss? Is this consistent with your recommendation in (1)? Why or why not? What other issues did you consider when making your recommendation?

2-35   In January 2009, **Harley-Davidson Inc.,** a manufacturer of motorcycles, said it would cut 1,100 jobs over two years (about 12% of its total work force) and close some plants as a result of recent declining sales. In addition, Harley said it would slash its production of motorcycles in 2009 by as much as 13% from already reduced 2008 levels. The 1,100 jobs to be cut over 2009 and 2010 included about 800 hourly production workers. Harley said most of the layoffs would occur in 2009.[c]

Required: (1) What effect would you expect the decision to have on Harley's break-even point? on the number of motorcycles Harley would have to sell to earn a desired profit?

(2) What nonfinancial issues do you think Harley's owners had to resolve in order to make this decision?

(3) What questions do you think the owners had to answer in order to resolve these issues?

2-36   Suppose you work for the Miniola Hills Bus Company. The company's 10 buses made a total of 80 trips per day on 310 days last year, for a total of 350,000 miles. Another year like last year will put the company out of business (and you out of a job!). Your boss has come to you for help. Last year, instead of earning a profit, the company lost $102,000, as shown here:

Revenue from riders (496,000 @ $0.50)		$248,000
Less operating costs:		
Depreciation on buses	$100,000	
Garage rent	20,000	
Licenses, fees, and insurance	40,000	
Maintenance	15,000	
Drivers' salaries	65,000	
Tires	20,000	
Gasoline and oil	90,000	(350,000)
Loss		($102,000)

Your boss is considering the following two plans for improving the company's profitability:

(a) Plan A—change the bus routes and reduce the number of trips to 60 per day in order to reduce the number of miles driven

(b) Plan B—sell bus tokens (five for $1.00) and student passes ($2.50 to ride all week) in order to increase the number of riders

Required: (1) Write your boss a memo discussing the effect that each of these plans might have on the costs and revenues of the bus company. Identify in your memo any assumptions you have made.

(2) If you were making this decision, what questions would you like answered before making the decision?

2-37 Yesterday, you received the following letter for your advice column in the local paper:

DR. DECISIVE

Dear Dr. Decisive:

What do you think about this situation? My boyfriend refuses to meet me for lunch until I admit I am wrong about this, which I'm NOT. The other day, when we went to lunch at Subs and Floats on campus, he noticed that they had raised the price of BLT subs. He got mad because he thinks the only reason they raised the price was to increase their profit. I told him that, first of all, their profit might not increase and that, second, he was basing his conclusion on some assumptions that might not be true and that if he would just *open up his mind,* he might see how those assumptions are affecting his conclusion. Well, *then* he got mad at *me.* I'm really upset because I know I'm right and because now I have to buy my own lunch. Will you please explain why I'm right? I know he'll listen to you (he reads your column daily). Until you answer, I'll be

"Starving."

Required: Meet with your Dr. Decisive team and write a response to "Starving."

ENDNOTES

[a] http://www.score.org/success_us_resources.html.

[b] http://www.usatoday.com/money/dotcoms/dot039.htm, http://www.usatoday.com/money/dotcoms/dot038.htm, http://faculty.msb.edu/homak/HomaHelpSite/WebHelp/Dot_coms__Dead_and_Mostly_Gone_Fortune_12-24-01.htm.

[c] http://money.cnn.com/2009/01/23/news/companies/harley_davidson.reut/index.htm.

DEVELOPING A BUSINESS PLAN:
BUDGETING

"ADVENTURE IS THE
RESULT OF POOR
PLANNING."

—COLONEL BLATCHFORD
SNELL

1 How does a budget contribute toward helping a company achieve its goals?

2 Do the activities of a company have a logical order that drives the organization of a budget?

3 What is the structure of the budgeting process, and how does a company begin that process?

4 What are the similarities and differences between a retail company's master budget and a service company's master budget?

5 After a company begins the budgeting process, is there a strategy it can use to complete the budget?

6 How can a manager use a budget to evaluate a company's performance and then use the results of that evaluation to influence the company's plans?

Unless you have been lucky enough to win the lottery, you probably have to budget your money. (Even if you *have* won the lottery, you probably want to budget your money.) Think for a minute about where you get your money. Do you receive cash from a job, a scholarship, financial aid, your parents, or some combination of these sources? Now think about where you spend your money. Most likely you spend it on day-to-day living expenses such as food, rent, utilities, and miscellaneous items, as well as on college-related costs such as tuition, fees, and books. Budgeting helps you to estimate when—and how much—cash will come in, and also helps you figure out when—and how much—cash you will need to pay out. With these estimates, you can plan your activities so that you have enough cash to pay for them.

 Suppose in budgeting your future cash payments, you realize that unless something changes, you will not have enough cash to pay your next car insurance bill. What alternatives do you have to solve this problem?

Companies must budget their resources too. For most companies, **budgeting** is a formal part of the ongoing planning process and periodically results in a set of related reports called *budgets*. A **budget** is a report that gives a financial description of one part of a company's planned activities for the budget period. For example, a budget might show how many products the company plans to sell during the next year, the dollar amount of these sales, and when the company will collect the cash from these sales. Another budget might show how much cash a company plans to spend during the same year renting business space, employing workers, and advertising its products, and also when the company plans to incur these costs.

WHY BUDGET?

Budgeting improves the planning, operating, and evaluating processes by helping an entrepreneur

- add discipline, or order, to the planning process,
- recognize and avoid potential operating problems,
- quantify plans, and
- create a "benchmark" for evaluating the company's performance.

I How does a budget contribute toward helping a company achieve its goals?

Budgeting Adds Discipline

Companies survive or fail because of the financial results of their activities. Therefore, *before implementing planning decisions,* effective entrepreneurs carefully think about what will happen as a result of these decisions. That's where budgeting comes in; the more complete and detailed the planning process is, the easier it is for an entrepreneur to foresee what might happen. Budgets add discipline because of their orderliness and detail.

FRANK'S
POTATO CONES
BAKED POTATO
IN A WAFFLE
CONE

OUT OF
BUSINESS

WWW.FMJN.US

© 2008 CARRILLO. DIST. BY UFS, INC.   10-23

How do you think a business plan could have helped this company?

Budgeting Highlights Potential Problems

Using budgeting to describe a company's plans allows the entrepreneur to uncover potential problems before they occur and to spot omissions or inconsistencies in the plans. For example, you and Anna may plan for Sweet Temptations to sell more boxes of chocolates in February than during other months because of expected Valentine's Day sales. Through the budgeting process, you may discover that unless something changes, Sweet Temptations will not have enough boxes of chocolates on hand in February to fill the expected customer orders. By seeing this problem ahead of time, you and Anna can adjust your purchase plans, perhaps preventing disappointed customers from having to go elsewhere to buy candy.

If you and Anna decide to purchase more chocolates in January and February because of expected increases in sales, Sweet Temptations will also have a higher bill from Unlimited Decadence. You and Anna will need to plan to have enough cash on hand to pay the bill when it is due. This plan will show up in the part of the budget that shows expected *purchases*. The budgeting process helps the entrepreneur see and evaluate how changes in plans affect different parts of a company's operations.

Budgeting Quantifies Plans

Business plans include the operating activities needed to meet the company's goals. A budget quantifies, or expresses in numbers, these operating activities and goals. For example, most companies have a goal of earning a specific profit for the budget year. This is stated in their business plans. Recall from Chapter 2 that Sweet Temptations included in its business plan a goal of earning a profit of $110 per month, or $1,320 ($110 $\times$ 12) during the coming year. The C-V-P analysis included in the business plan in Chapter 2 indicates that to earn this profit, Sweet Temptations must have monthly sales averaging 720 boxes of chocolates, so during the year it must sell at least 8,640 boxes (720 $\times$ 12) of chocolates. Sweet Temptations' budget will indicate how many boxes of chocolates it plans to sell each month of the year to meet its profit goal and how many boxes it must purchase each month to support its projected sales.

Budgeting also quantifies the resources that the company expects to use for its planned sales and purchasing activities. For example, if Sweet Temptations must purchase 900 boxes of chocolates to cover its expected sales for any given month, the budget will indicate how much (and when) Sweet Temptations expects to pay for these chocolates.

Budgeting Creates Benchmarks

Since budgets help quantify plans, an entrepreneur also uses budgets as "benchmarks." The entrepreneur periodically compares the results of the company's actual operating activities with the related budget amounts. These comparisons measure the company's progress toward achieving its goals and help the entrepreneur evaluate how efficiently the company is using its resources. The comparisons also help the entrepreneur focus on what changes should be made, if any, to bring the company's operating activities more in line with its goals. To save time and effort, the entrepreneur uses a management principle known as **management by exception**. Under this principle, the entrepreneur focuses on improving the activities that show significant differences (or exceptions) between budgeted and actual results. These activities have the greatest potential for positively influencing the company's operations.

OPERATING CYCLES

2 Do the activities of a company have a logical order that drives the organization of a budget?

Earlier, we referred to the operating activities of a company. The operating activities of a company depend on whether it is a retail, service, or manufacturing company because each of these different types of companies has a different operating cycle. In budgeting, a company quantifies its planned activities in relation to its operating cycle. This process is similar to when you prepare your personal budget for the semester. Before we get into the details of budgeting, we will briefly discuss the operating cycles of retail and service companies. We will discuss the operating cycle of a manufacturing company in Chapter 11.

The Operating Cycle of a Retail Company

A **retail company's operating cycle** is the average time it takes the company to use cash to buy goods for sale (called *inventory*), to sell these goods to customers, and to collect cash from its customers. Sweet Temptations' operating cycle is the time it takes to pay cash to purchase boxes of chocolates from Unlimited Decadence, to sell these chocolates to customers, and to collect the cash from the customers. Unlimited Decadence allows Sweet Temptations to "charge" its purchases of boxes of chocolates. From Sweet Temptations' point of view, these are called *credit purchases* and result in *accounts payable*. Similarly, although most of Sweet Temptations' sales are cash sales, it also allows some of its customers to "charge" their purchases of chocolates. (These purchases are made on "charge accounts" set up directly between the customers and Sweet Temptations; they are not made on charge cards such as VISA or Discover.) From Sweet Temptations' point of view, sales to these customers are called *credit sales* and result in *accounts receivable*.

 From the customers' point of view, what do you think Sweet Temptations' credit sales to them are called?

Sweet Temptations will pay cash for its accounts payable to Unlimited Decadence within 30 days of the purchases. Similarly, Sweet Temptations will collect cash from customers' accounts receivable within a few days after their purchases of chocolates. We will talk more about how a company decides to extend credit to customers later in this chapter and in Chapter 8.

Exhibit 3-1 shows Sweet Temptations' operating cycle. As you will see later, Sweet Temptations' budgeting process quantifies its operating cycle and its other activities.

The Operating Cycle of a Service Company

Service companies have a budgeting process that is very similar to that of retail companies. One major difference between these two types of companies, however, involves their operating cycles. A **service company's operating cycle** is the average time it takes the company to use cash to acquire supplies and services, to sell the services to customers, and to collect cash from its customers.

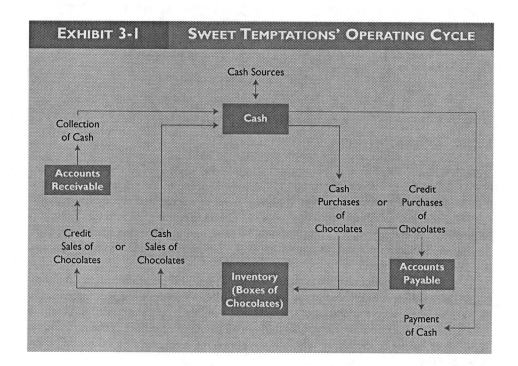

EXHIBIT 3-1   SWEET TEMPTATIONS' OPERATING CYCLE

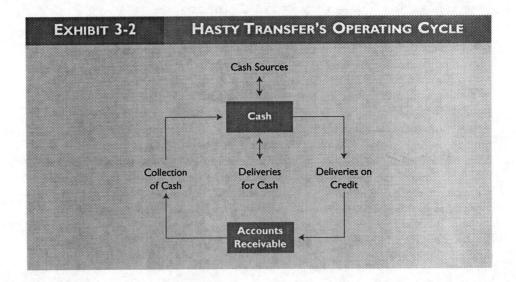

EXHIBIT 3-2   HASTY TRANSFER'S OPERATING CYCLE

Exhibit 3-2 shows the operating cycle of Hasty Transfer Company, a shipping company hired by Unlimited Decadence to ship its chocolates to Sweet Temptations and other retail companies around the country. This operating cycle may be shorter than that of a retail company because there is no inventory to purchase.

The operating cycle for some service companies can be much longer than the cycle for most retail companies because for these service companies, one service, or job, can take months or years. For example, think about the life of some of the advertising campaigns you have observed recently. For instance, the Energizer Bunny (batteries) and Tony the Tiger (cereal) have been around for years (or decades). Many service companies with long jobs try to shorten their operating cycles by periodically collecting payments from their customers for completed segments of the work. Hasty Transfer's operating cycle, on the other hand, could average only two or three days, since it delivers perishable candy to companies in the same city in which Unlimited Decadence's factory is located and also to companies around the country. The length of Hasty Transfer's operating cycle depends on Hasty's collection policies and when it expects to be paid by its customers. Like Sweet Temptations, Hasty Transfer quantifies its operating cycle and other activities in a budget.

 How long do you think a university's or college's operating cycle is? What are the components of its operating cycle?

THE BUDGET AS A FRAMEWORK FOR PLANNING

3 What is the structure of the budgeting process, and how does a company begin that process?

Budgeting is most useful in decision-making when it is organized to show different aspects of operations. The master budget is the overall structure a company uses to organize its budgeting process. A **master budget** is a set of interrelated reports (or budgets) showing the relationships among a company's (1) goals to be met, (2) activities to be performed in its operating cycle, (3) resources to be used, and (4) expected financial results. A company includes the master budget with the C-V-P analysis in the financial plan section of its business plan.

The individual budgets in the master budget may be different from company to company. These differences are due to the number of different products each company sells, the varying sizes and complexities of the companies and their operations, and whether the companies are retail, service, or manufacturing companies. Regardless of the differences, each master budget describes the relationships between a company's goals, activities, resources, and results.

© PHOTOPIA

The "Tony the Tiger" advertising campaign has been around for decades. Do you think the agency's operating cycle is *that* long?

A master budget for a retail company usually includes the following budgets and projected financial statements:

1. Sales budget
2. Purchases budget
3. Selling expenses budget
4. General and administrative expenses budget
5. Cash budget (projected cash flow statement)
6. Projected income statement
7. Projected balance sheet

A service company's master budget does not include a purchases budget and usually combines the expenses budgets. A manufacturing company's master budget includes additional budgets related to its manufacturing activities.

A company prepares its annual master budget for a year or more into the future. It breaks the master budget down by each budget period—generally by quarter (three-month period). Within each quarter, it shows the budget information on a monthly basis. Some companies develop budgets for each department which they then combine to form a master budget. For example, **JCPenney** might develop budgets for apparel, for housewares, for bed and bath accessories, for optical departments, and for styling salons.

4 What are the similarities and differences between a retail company's master budget and a service company's master budget?

Exhibit 3-3 shows (with arrows) the important relationships among the reports in Sweet Temptations' master budget. Notice that the last budgets prepared in a company's budgeting process are the projected financial statements for the budget period: the cash budget (also called a *projected cash flow statement*), the projected income statement, and the projected balance sheet. The projected financial statements give managers a "preview" of what the company's actual financial statements should look like at the end of the budget period *if everything goes according to plan.* The information for these projected financial statements comes from the other budgets.

We will discuss the nature and the relationships of Sweet Temptations' budgets to illustrate how a retail company plans and describes its operating activities. Since Sweet Temptations is a small company, the illustrations will be simple. The larger a company is, the more complex and detailed its budget reports must be to be useful. Often, though,

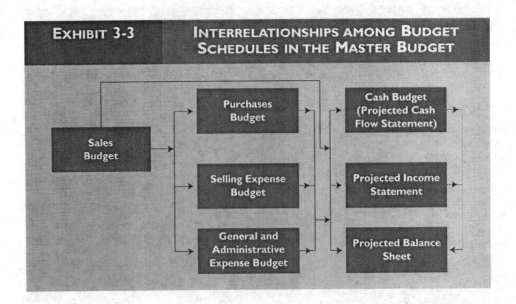

managers of large companies prepare summaries similar to the simpler budgets that we use in this chapter.

When you look at the budgets for Sweet Temptations, try to understand the logic of their development and how they interrelate. As you study the budgets, remember the following "start-up" information from Chapter 2. During December 2010 Anna plans to

- invest $15,000 in Sweet Temptations,
- rent store space for $1,000 per month, paying $6,000 in advance for six months' rent,
- buy $1,800 of store equipment by making a $1,000 down payment and signing a note payable for the remaining amount,
- order 360 boxes of chocolates from Unlimited Decadence for $1,620, to be paid for in January 2011,
- purchase and pay for $700 of supplies.

For each budget, we will also briefly discuss the similar budget for Hasty Transfer, a service company.

The Sales Budget

5 After a company begins the budgeting process, is there a strategy it can use to complete the budget?

The budgeting process begins with the sales budget because product sales or service contracts affect all the other operating activities of a company. (Without sales of chocolates, why would Sweet Temptations be in business? Without arrangements with Unlimited Decadence and other companies to ship chocolates and other goods, why would Hasty Transfer exist?) A retail company without sales would not need employees, inventory, retail space, store equipment, supplies, advertising, or utilities. As you will soon see, the same is true for a service company. For this reason, the sales budget affects all of the other budgets.

The Retail Company's Sales Budget

For a retail company, the **sales budget** shows the number of units of inventory that the company expects to sell each month, the related monthly sales revenue, and in which months the company expects to collect cash from these sales. To estimate the number of units of inventory it will sell in each month, a company gathers various types of information, such as past sales data, industry trends, and economic forecasts. If Sweet Temptations were an older company, you and Anna might analyze Sweet Temptations' past sales trends to get an idea about what sales level to expect for the future. However, you should also consider the current economic conditions or circumstances that affect the candy industry.

For example, if the economy has worsened and people are struggling to get food on the table, customers may view the purchase of chocolates as a luxury, and sales may drop, regardless of the level of past sales. On the other hand, if the economy is improving, people may have extra income to spend (extra disposable income), and sales of candy may increase. New findings and breakthroughs also can affect sales. For example, in the past several years, studies comparing test subjects who ate dark chocolate with those who ate milk chocolate found that those who ate dark chocolate had a significant drop in their blood pressure, while the others did not. They also found that those who ate dark chocolate had the most antioxidants in their blood after eating the chocolate.[a] Market analysts said that in the two years after the studies' results were released, sales of dark chocolates *doubled* in Great Britain! While this was good news for the chocolate confectioners, the overall sales in their chocolate market which had been declining, increased by only 10%.[b]

How do you think a well-publicized discovery that sugar is actually good for people would affect your prediction of candy sales for next year?

Market analysts or consultants are another source of information about the estimated number of products to be sold. Although Anna has a marketing degree, she is busy getting the company "up and running." Therefore, she has hired Joe Smiley (see Exhibit 2-2) to study the market for boxed chocolates in the area north of the metroplex and provide an analysis, including a report on the effect that different prices would have on potential sales of the chocolates. Joe's research should help Anna predict sales during Sweet Temptations' first year of operations. Large companies have additional sources of market information, including their sales forces as well as marketing and advertising specialists. We will discuss the sources in Chapter 11.

After a company has estimated the amount of inventory it expects to sell, it determines its estimated sales revenue by multiplying the number of units of inventory it expects to sell by the unit selling price. After computing its monthly estimated sales revenue, the company determines how much cash it expects to collect each month from sales. If all sales are cash sales, the cash to be collected each month is equal to the sales revenue of that month. For most companies, however, a portion (sometimes substantial) of their sales are credit sales. If a company allows credit sales, its cash collections of accounts receivable will lag behind its sales revenues.

What do you think is the difference between cash sales and sales revenue? Are they the same thing?

The credit-granting policy of a company can have a great impact on the length of time between the sale of its product and the collection of cash from that sale. You and Anna would certainly not grant credit to a customer with a poor credit history because there would be a good chance that the customer either will pay you a long time after the sale, pay you only part of the bill, or not pay you at all. Many companies spend a lot of time and effort studying the paying habits of their customers and deciding on an appropriate credit-granting policy. The goal is to shorten the time between sales and collections of cash, and reduce the risk of not being able to collect from their customers. At the same time, companies don't want an overly restrictive credit policy that discourages customers from buying on credit.

What information about a customer do you think would be helpful in Sweet Temptations' decision of whether or not to grant the customer credit?

Anna has decided to grant credit to a few nearby companies, hoping they will make numerous purchases. To start, Anna estimates that these credit sales will be about 5 percent of total sales. She has also decided to give these credit customers terms of n/10 ("net 10"), which means that they will pay Sweet Temptations within ten days of when they make credit purchases. Anna selected n/10 because Sweet Temptations is a new company and she does not think it should wait more than ten days to receive cash from its credit customers. Because of this policy, Sweet Temptations will collect roughly two-thirds of each month's credit sales in the month of the sales and the remaining one-third of the credit sales in the following month.

Exhibit 3-4 shows the relationship between Sweet Temptations' January credit sales and its cash collections from these sales. This diagram shows that the sales revenue is earned at the time of the credit sale. However, the cash collection from the credit sale occurs ten days after the sale takes place. As you can see in the exhibit, cash collections from January credit sales occur partly in January and partly in February. For instance, the cash collections from the January 1 credit sales occur on about January 11, and the cash collections from the credit sales on January 31 occur on about February 10.

Exhibit 3-5 shows the sales budget of Sweet Temptations for the first quarter of 2011. The sales amounts are based on Joe Smiley's market analysis. Notice that it shows budgeted sales for each month both in units (boxes of chocolates) and in dollars of sales revenue, and that the monthly sales amounts are added across to show the quarter totals (2,460 units; $24,600 sales revenue). Also notice that the sales budget divides total sales each month between cash sales and credit sales.

 How do you think dividing total monthly sales between cash sales and credit sales helps in the creation of the rest of the sales budget?

The Service Company's Sales Budget

The sales budget of a service company is very similar to the sales budget of a retail company, except that the former is selling services rather than products. When Hasty Transfer budgets its sales, it is budgeting sales of delivery services. Expected cash collections from customers depend on Hasty's collection policies. For example, Hasty may expect to be paid by its customers when it picks up merchandise the customers want to ship. On the other hand, Hasty may expect to be paid by its customers only after it delivers the customers' merchandise. Furthermore, Hasty may grant credit to some of its customers— a policy that also will affect the timing of its cash receipts.

EXHIBIT 3-4	RELATIONSHIP BETWEEN CREDIT SALES AND CASH COLLECTIONS

Date of:	January	February
Sales Revenues	1 2 3 4 5 6 7 8 9 10 11 12 13 14 15 16 17 18 19 20 21 22 23 24 25 26 27 28 29 30 31	
Cash Collections	11 12 13 14 15 16 17 18 19 20 21 22 23 24 25 26 27 28 29 30 31	1 2 3 4 5 6 7 8 9 10

EXHIBIT 3-5	SALES BUDGET

SWEET TEMPTATIONS
Sales Budget
First Quarter 2011

	January	February	March	Quarter
Budgeted total unit sales				
(boxes of chocolates)	720	1,200	540	2,460
Budgeted selling price per box	$ 10	$ 10	$ 10	$ 10
Budgeted total sales revenue	$7,200	$12,000	$5,400	$24,600
Budgeted cash sales				
(95% of total sales revenue)	$6,840	$11,400	$5,130	$23,370
Budgeted credit sales				
(5% of total sales revenue)	360	600	270	1,230
Budgeted total sales revenue	$7,200	$12,000	$5,400	$24,600
Expected cash collections:				
From cash sales	$6,840	$11,400	$5,130	$23,370
From January credit sales	240[a]	120[a]		360
From February credit sales		400[a]	200[a]	600
From March credit sales			180[a]	180
Total cash collections	$7,080	$11,920	$5,510	$24,510

[a]Sweet Temptations estimates that it will collect two-thirds of each month's credit sales during the month of sale. It will collect the remaining one-third in the month following the sale.

Years ago, a new airline called Air South began flying from Jacksonville, Florida, to Atlanta, Georgia. The fare for the trip at that time was $19 plus a first-class stamp. How do you think Air South budgeted its cash receipts? How do you think Air South is doing now?

Seasonal Sales

Some companies' sales occur evenly throughout the year. Other companies experience *seasonal sales*. That is, these companies' customers purchase the inventory or services more often in some months than in others. The sale of ski apparel is an example of seasonal sales. Although ski shops sell some ski apparel throughout the year, most of their sales occur right before and during ski season. A company offering skiing lessons (a service) may not even be open during the summer. The sale of candy is not as extreme, but it does have some seasonality. For Sweet Temptations, monthly sales differences during its first quarter reflect an expected increase in sales as Valentine's Day approaches.

What other seasonal effects would you expect for Sweet Temptations?

The Retail Company's Purchases Budget

Once a company has estimated (budgeted) its unit sales for each month of the quarter, it can determine the best approach for purchasing the needed inventory. Sweet Temptations expects to sell 2,460 boxes of chocolates this quarter (from the sales budget in Exhibit 3-5). You may be wondering how many of those boxes Sweet Temptations should be ordering now. In making this purchase decision, you should consider several factors.

First, there are the costs of keeping the company's money invested in inventory (rather than investing it somewhere else), of storing and handling inventory, and of paying for insurance and taxes on inventory. Higher inventory levels also increase the risk of theft, damage, and obsolescence. If Sweet Temptations holds too many boxes of chocolates, you and Anna risk either selling chocolates that are not fresh and losing future customers, or having to throw away old chocolates. (Or, with more chocolates around, you may be more tempted to eat the inventory!) Also, there is a physical limit to the number of boxes you can stock in the candy store. For these reasons, some companies use "just-in-time" (JIT) inventory systems, in which they purchase inventory a day before they need it. We will discuss JIT inventory systems in Chapter 17 of Volume 2.

On the other hand, it also can be very expensive not to carry enough inventory. For example, if Sweet Temptations starts running low on chocolates, it may have to pay Hasty Transfer higher shipping costs for rush orders or pay Unlimited Decadence higher costs per box for smaller, last-minute orders. You may also risk alienating customers if you run out of inventory. Every company must plan its own inventory levels, considering the costs of both carrying and not carrying inventory and trying to keep the combined total at the lowest possible amount. Even though the purchases budget does not address all of the above factors, it will help you and Anna make the best purchase decision.

The **purchases budget** shows the purchases (in units) required in each month to make the expected sales (from the sales budget) in that month and to keep inventory at desired levels. It also shows the costs of these purchases and the expected timing and amount of the cash payments for these purchases.

Frequently, companies set desired end-of-month inventory levels at either a constant percentage of the following month's budgeted unit sales or at large enough levels to meet future sales for a specified time. Since many companies base their purchase orders on sales *estimates,* they want to have extra inventory available to sell in case they have underestimated their sales or in case their next shipment of inventory arrives later than expected.

Anna plans to order chocolates from Unlimited Decadence once every month. She has also decided that during any month, Sweet Temptations should have enough candy on hand to cover that month's candy sales and also to have an ending inventory large enough to cover one-half of the next month's sales. For example, projected sales for the first quarter of 2011 (from the sales budget in Exhibit 3-5) and for April (from projections for the second quarter) are as follows:

	January	February	March	April
Budgeted total unit sales (boxes of chocolates)	720	1,200	540	900

Based on Anna's purchasing policy, Sweet Temptations must have enough inventory during January to equal budgeted sales for January plus one-half of budgeted sales for February, or 1,320 boxes of chocolates [720 boxes + $^1/_2$ (1,200)]. (Then, if Sweet Temptations sells 720 boxes during January, it will have inventory at the end of January equal to half of February's budgeted sales.) Since Sweet Temptations will start business in January with the 360 boxes of chocolates purchased in December ($^1/_2$ of the 720 January budgeted sales), January purchases must be 960 boxes (1,320 total boxes needed − 360 boxes already on hand). Sweet Temptations uses the same calculations to determine each month's purchases of boxes of chocolates. Exhibit 3-6 illustrates how budgeted purchases and budgeted sales are linked together for the first quarter of the year.

 What do you think are the advantages of Anna's plans to order chocolates once per month rather than more often?

Normally, Sweet Temptations will make purchases during the first week of each month and will receive delivery of the purchases at the beginning of the second week of the month. However, since Sweet Temptations will open for business in January, it must purchase 360 boxes of chocolates in mid-December so that they will be available to sell on

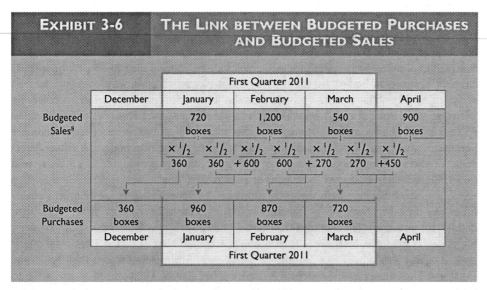

EXHIBIT 3-6	THE LINK BETWEEN BUDGETED PURCHASES AND BUDGETED SALES			

aFrom Exhibit 3-5, except April, which was estimated as part of second-quarter projections.

the first day of business in January. No sales of chocolates will occur in December, so the amount of chocolates that Sweet Temptations purchases in December will still be in Sweet Temptations' inventory at the end of December (and at the beginning of January).

Exhibit 3-7 shows the purchases budget of Sweet Temptations for the first quarter of 2011. Remember that Sweet Temptations wants to purchase enough boxes of chocolates

EXHIBIT 3-7	PURCHASES BUDGET			

SWEET TEMPTATIONS
Purchases Budget
First Quarter 2011

	January	February	March	Quarter
Budgeted total unit sales (boxes of chocolates)	720	1,200	540	2,460
Add: Desired ending inventory of boxes of chocolates[a]	600	270	450[b]	450[c]
Total boxes of chocolates required	1,320	1,470	990	2,910
Less: Beginning inventory of boxes of chocolates[d]	(360)[e]	(600)	(270)	(360)[f]
Budgeted purchases of boxes of chocolates	960	870	720	2,550
Purchase price per box of chocolates	$ 4.50	$ 4.50	$ 4.50	$ 4.50
Cost of purchases	$4,320	$3,915	$3,240	$11,475
Cash payments for purchases	$1,620[e]	$4,320	$3,915	$ 9,855

aThe desired ending inventory is 1/2 of next month's budgeted sales.
bApril's budgeted sales are 900 boxes of chocolates.
cThe desired ending inventory at the end of the quarter is the same as the desired ending inventory at the end of March (which is the end of the quarter).
dThe beginning inventory is the same as the previous month's ending inventory.
e360 boxes of chocolates, at a total purchase price of $1,620, ordered in December 2010 to prepare for the start of business.
fThe quarter's beginning inventory is the same as December's ending inventory (January's beginning inventory).

each month to meet budgeted sales during the month and to have enough boxes left at the end of the month to cover one-half of the next month's sales. These boxes must come from the inventory on hand at the beginning of the month and from any purchases that the company makes during the month. By subtracting the budgeted beginning inventory from the total inventory required for any given month, you can determine how many purchases (in boxes) to budget for that month. Since purchases are a *variable* cost, the cost of boxes of chocolates purchased is determined by multiplying the number of boxes by $4.50 per unit. Since Sweet Temptations has an agreement with Unlimited Decadence to pay for its purchases within 30 days after the purchases, the payment for each month's purchase is budgeted for the following month. For instance, the budgeted January purchase of 960 boxes of chocolates costing $4.50 per box amounts to a total purchase cost of $4,320, which is budgeted to be paid in February.

Companies that purchase their inventories from suppliers in other countries sometimes pay for their purchases in the other countries' currencies (yen or pesos rather than dollars, for example). These companies should budget their purchases in dollars, however. Suppose, for example, that Sweet Temptations purchased boxes of chocolates from a Belgian company instead of from Unlimited Decadence. Since Belgium is a member of the European Union that uses a currency called a *euro,* Sweet Temptations would have to convert euros to dollars when preparing its purchases budget.

Remember that budgets represent a company's *plans* and are based on estimates. As new information becomes available, the company sometimes changes its plans.

 Suppose that January sales turn out to be 1,010 boxes of chocolates. Should Sweet Temptations change its plans for February and March? What questions should you ask before deciding whether the plans should change, which part of the plans should change, and by how much?

The Retail Company's Selling Expenses Budget

To sell its inventory, a retail company must engage in selling activities. The **selling expenses budget** shows the expenses and related cash payments associated with planned selling activities. Examples of selling expenses include salespeople's salaries and commissions, store rent, and advertising. Each of these expenses directly relates to sales.

A selling expenses budget is developed by reviewing past selling expenses (if they are available) and then adjusting them for current plans. It is important for the entrepreneur to understand prior cost behavior patterns when creating a selling expenses budget because some selling expenses are *variable* and change directly with the amount of inventory sold whereas some remain *fixed* regardless of the sales volume. By applying these behavior patterns, the entrepreneur can predict what each selling expense will be at a given estimated sales volume. Sales commissions are an example of variable selling expenses, since total sales commissions increase in direct proportion to increases in sales. Store rent and advertising, on the other hand, are fixed selling expenses, in many cases, because total rent and advertising expenses stay the same as sales increase during the period. In developing a selling expenses budget, the entrepreneur should also be able to distinguish selling expenses from general and administrative expenses. Sometimes fixed expenses must be allocated on a reasonable basis between the two types of expenses.

Exhibit 3-8 shows the selling expenses budget for Sweet Temptations for the first quarter of 2011. The January expenses are the same items listed in Exhibit 2-8 in Chapter 2. These expenses are all *fixed* expenses, so Sweet Temptations expects them to be the same in all three months. (Remember, though, that selling expenses also can be variable expenses.) Not all the *amounts* from Exhibit 2-8 are related to selling activities, however. You and Anna have estimated that three-fourths of each of the following expenses is tied directly to selling activities. The other one-fourth of each expense is tied to the administrative activities of Sweet Temptations and will be included in the general and adminis-

EXHIBIT 3-8	SELLING EXPENSES BUDGET

SWEET TEMPTATIONS
Selling Expenses Budget
First Quarter 2011

	January	February	March	Quarter
Budgeted selling expenses:[a]				
Rent expense	$ 750.00	$ 750.00	$ 750.00	$2,250.00
Salaries expense	1,537.50	1,537.50	1,537.50	4,612.50
Consulting expense	150.00	150.00	150.00	450.00
Advertising expense	305.00	305.00	305.00	915.00
Supplies expense	22.50	22.50	22.50	67.50
Depreciation expense:				
Store equipment	15.00	15.00	15.00	45.00
Telephone and utilities expense	187.50	187.50	187.50	562.50
Total budgeted selling expenses	$2,967.50	$2,967.50	$2,967.50	$8,902.50
Budgeted cash payments for selling expenses[b]	$2,180.00	$2,180.00	$2,180.00	$6,540.00

[a]Exhibit 2-8 shows Sweet Temptations' projected expenses for the month of January. Since these are *fixed* expenses, they are expected to be the same for February and March.
[b]The $787.50 ($2,967.50 − $2,180) difference between the total budgeted selling expenses and budgeted cash payments for selling expenses each month occurs because the expenses for rent, supplies, and depreciation ($750 + $22.50 + $15) relate to Sweet Temptations' planned December expenditures for rent, supplies, and equipment. They are not counted again as cash payments.

trative expenses budget. These expenses are allocated to the selling expenses budget as follows:

Rent	$1,000 × 3/4 = $ 750.00
Salaries	$2,050 × 3/4 = $1,537.50
Consulting	$ 200 × 3/4 = $ 150.00
Supplies	$ 30 × 3/4 = $ 22.50
Telephone and utilities	$ 250 × 3/4 = $ 187.50

Like the purchases budget, the selling expenses budget includes a schedule of budgeted cash payments for each month in the budget period. The company's payment policies and how they apply to the individual expenses determine the budgeted cash payments.

For now, Sweet Temptations' payment policy is to pay for all of its expenses (except rent, supplies, and depreciation) in the month in which they occur. However, if its policy were to make payments in the month following the expenses, the cash payment schedule of the selling expenses budget would resemble the cash collection schedule illustrated in the sales budget in Exhibit 3-5. Notice that there is a $787.50 ($2,967.50 − $2,180) difference between the budgeted total selling expenses each month and the budgeted monthly cash payments for these expenses. This is because Sweet Temptations expects to pay cash in advance for six months' rent, purchase supplies with cash, and make a cash down payment to buy store equipment in December 2010 to get ready to open for business. The $787.50 ($750 rent expense + $22.50 supplies expense + $15 depreciation expense) monthly expenses related to these planned December cash expenditures are not counted again as planned cash payments in January, February, or March.

The Retail Company's General and Administrative Expenses Budget

For a retail company, the **general and administrative expenses budget** shows the expenses and related cash payments associated with expected activities other than selling.

EXHIBIT 3-9	GENERAL AND ADMINISTRATIVE EXPENSES BUDGET		

SWEET TEMPTATIONS
General and Administrative Expenses Budget
First Quarter 2011

	January	February	March	Quarter
Budgeted general and administrative expenses^a				
Rent expense	$ 250.00	$ 250.00	$ 250.00	$ 750.00
Salaries expense	512.50	512.50	512.50	1,537.50
Consulting expense	50.00	50.00	50.00	150.00
Supplies expense	7.50	7.50	7.50	22.50
Telephone and utilities expense	62.50	62.50	62.50	187.50
Total budgeted general and administrative expenses	$ 882.50	$ 882.50	$ 882.50	$2,647.50
Budgeted cash payments for general and administrative expenses^b	$ 625.00	$ 625.00	$ 625.00	$1,875.00

^aExhibit 2-8 shows Sweet Temptations' projected expenses for the month of January. Since these are fixed expenses, Sweet Temptations expects them to be the same for February and March.
^bThe $257.50 ($882.50 − $625) difference between the total budgeted general and administrative expenses and the budgeted cash payments for these expenses each month occurs because the monthly expenses ($250 + $7.50) related to the planned December cash expenditures for rent and supplies are not counted again as cash payments.

Examples of general and administrative expenses are secretaries' salaries, consulting charges, and the cost of renting office space. To prepare the general and administrative expenses budget, the entrepreneur reviews past expenses (if they are available), identifies them as fixed or variable, and adjusts them for current plans.

Exhibit 3-9 shows the general and administrative expenses budget for Sweet Temptations for the first quarter of 2011. These expenses are all *fixed* expenses, although general and administrative expenses can also be variable expenses. As we discussed earlier, Sweet Temptations allocates the total of certain monthly expenses between selling activities and general and administrative activities. Recall that you and Anna estimated that one-fourth of each of the expenses is tied directly to administrative activities. The other three-fourths of each is tied to sales activities and appears on the selling expenses budget. These expenses are allocated to the general and administrative expenses budget as follows:

Rent	$1,000 × 1/4 = $250.00
Salaries	$2,050 × 1/4 = $512.50
Consulting	$ 200 × 1/4 = $ 50.00
Supplies	$ 30 × 1/4 = $ 7.50
Telephone and utilities	$ 250 × 1/4 = $ 62.50

Like the selling expenses budget, the general and administrative expenses budget includes a schedule of budgeted cash payments for each month in the budget period. These cash payments are determined according to the company's payment policies. Sweet Temptations plans to pay for all the expenses listed on the general and administrative expenses budget in the month they occur except for rent and supplies, which it paid for in December.

The Service Company's Expenses Budget

Service companies do not have a purchases budget for inventory, since they are selling a service rather than a product. Also, they usually do not divide their budgeted expenses into two different budgets, one for selling expenses and one for general and administrative expenses. Instead, in budgeting expenses, service companies simply prepare an *operating expenses* budget.

Remember that our discussion of cost behaviors in Chapter 2 noted that variable costs vary in total in direct proportion to volume. *Volume* can refer to a variety of activities. One measure of volume used by retail companies is number of unit sales. Because they are selling a service, though, service companies are very labor-intensive. Salaries are a major expense for these companies, and many of their other expenses vary with the number of hours that the employees work. Therefore, many service companies use the number of hours that employees work as a measure of volume. Regardless, service companies have many of the same fixed expenses that retail companies have, such as rent and advertising.

Cash Management and the Cash Budget

The way a company manages its cash can make the difference between success and failure. Cash management involves keeping an eye on the company's cash balance to make sure that

1. there is enough cash on hand to pay for planned operations during the current period,
2. there is a "cash buffer" on hand, and
3. there is not too much cash on hand.

An insufficient cash balance can cause a problem for a company. Without enough cash, a company will have trouble operating at a normal level and paying its bills. In the most extreme case, an entrepreneur will not be able to operate the company at all because it will have gone out of business. Therefore, a good entrepreneur is always looking for long- and short-term financing sources, such as lines of credit at a bank that allow the company to borrow money "as needed" and loan guarantees from government agencies such as the **U.S. Small Business Administration**. A good entrepreneur also watches the company's cash balance to determine when to pay back the financing. We will discuss short-term financing again in Chapter 13 and long-term financing in Chapter 22 of Volume 2.

A cash buffer means having some extra cash on hand (or available through a line of credit) to cover normal, but unexpected, events. For example, an unexpected surge in candy sales would cause Sweet Temptations to have to purchase more inventory than planned. A cash buffer would help cover that purchase. A company's insurance policy would usually cover abnormal and unexpected events such as natural disasters or fires.

Too much cash on hand may seem like an odd problem to have because almost everyone would like to have more cash. An excessive cash balance is a problem for a company, though, because this cash balance is not productive. That is, cash earns nothing for the company unless the company invests it internally in profitable projects, or externally in an interest-bearing account or in government or business securities that earn dividends or interest. Therefore, a successful entrepreneur continually watches for good investment opportunities—even short-run opportunities. We will discuss short-term and long-term investments in Chapter 23 of Volume 2.

The Retail Company's Cash Budget (Projected Cash Flow Statement)

The **cash budget** shows the company's expected cash receipts and payments, and how they affect the company's cash balance. The cash budget is very important in cash management. It helps the entrepreneur anticipate cash shortages, thus avoiding the problems of having too little cash on hand to operate and to pay its bills. This budget also helps the company avoid having excess cash that could be better used for profitable projects or investments.

Besides helping the entrepreneur anticipate cash shortages and excesses, the cash budget can also help external users. For example, a potential lender (such as a bank) may want to evaluate the company's cash budget to see how the company plans to use the borrowed cash and to anticipate when the company will have enough cash to repay the loan.

A company's cash budget is similar in many respects to the cash flow statement we discussed in Chapter 1. However, the cash budget shows the cash receipts (inflows) and cash payments (outflows) that the company *expects* as a result of its plans (which is why it sometimes is called a *projected cash flow statement*). On the other hand, a company's cash flow statement reports its *actual* cash receipts and payments. Like the cash flow statement (see Exhibit 1-10), a cash budget may have three sections: it always has an *operating activities* section, and if the company plans for investing or financing activities, the cash budget will have separate *investing activities* and *financing activities* sections.

The **operating activities section** of the cash budget summarizes the cash receipts and payments the company expects as a result of its planned operations. These expected cash flows come from the sales, purchases, and expenses budgets we discussed earlier. This section also shows the net cash inflows (excess of cash receipts over cash payments) or the net cash outflows (excess of cash payments over cash receipts) expected from operations. Adding the net cash inflows to the beginning cash balance (or subtracting the net cash outflows) results in the expected cash balance from operations at the end of the budget period.

The **investing activities section** of the cash budget—if needed—shows the cash payments and receipts the company expects from planned investing activities. A company's investing activities include, for instance, purchases or sales of land, buildings, and equipment, or investments in the stocks and bonds of governments or other companies.

 Why do you think cash receipts from the sale of land, buildings, and equipment, as well as from dividends received on investments, are included in the investing section of the cash budget?

Although investing activities can occur at any time, companies usually have policies about investing cash balances on hand in excess of a predetermined amount. For instance, based on planned operating activities, Anna has decided that Sweet Temptations should invest any cash on hand in excess of $15,000 in any month.

The **financing activities section** of the cash budget—if needed—shows the cash receipts and payments the company expects from planned financing activities. A company's financing activities include borrowings and repayments of loans, investments by owners, and withdrawals by owners. The cash budget helps a manager decide when financing activities will be necessary. For example, in considering the need for a cash buffer, Anna has decided that Sweet Temptations will begin financing activities when its cash balance drops below $7,000.

Exhibit 3-10 shows Sweet Temptations' cash budget for the first quarter of 2011. Notice that Sweet Temptations' cash budget summarizes the receipts and payments that you saw in the budgets we discussed earlier. The cash receipts amounts come from the sales budget, and the cash payments amounts come from the purchases budget, the selling expenses budget, and the general and administrative expenses budget. The $7,300 beginning cash balance for January (and the quarter) is Sweet Temptations' cash balance at the end of December, assuming preparations for the start of business go according to plan. The ending cash balance for each month is also the beginning cash balance for the next month.

Sweet Temptations has no investment activities planned for this quarter since the expected cash balances in the first three months of 2011 are not more than $15,000. Also, none of the monthly cash balances during the quarter are less than $7,000, so no financing activities are planned during this quarter. Thus, Sweet Temptations' cash budget does not include an investing activities or a financing activities section. We will discuss planned cash flows from both investing and financing activities in Chapter 11.

The Service Company's Cash Budget (Projected Cash Flow Statement)

The cash budget of a service company is similar to that of a retail company except that the service company reports cash flow information that is obtained from fewer budgets.

EXHIBIT 3-10	CASH BUDGET (PROJECTED CASH FLOW STATEMENT)

SWEET TEMPTATIONS
Cash Budget
First Quarter 2011

	January	February	March	Quarter
Cash flow from operating activities:				
Cash receipts from sales[a]	$7,080.00	$11,920.00	$ 5,510.00	$24,510.00
Cash payments for:				
Purchases[b]	$1,620.00	$ 4,320.00	$ 3,915.00	$ 9,855.00
Selling expenses[c]	2,180.00	2,180.00	2,180.00	6,540.00
General and administrative expenses[d]	625.00	625.00	625.00	1,875.00
Total payments	$4,425.00	$ 7,125.00	$ 6,720.00	$18,270.00
Net cash inflow (outflow) from operations	$2,655.00	$ 4,795.00	$(1,210.00)	$ 6,240.00
Add: Beginning cash balance	7,300.00	9,955.00	14,750.00	7,300.00
Ending cash balance from operations	$9,955.00	$14,750.00	$13,540.00	$13,540.00

[a]From sales budget (Exhibit 3-5)
[b]From purchases budget (Exhibit 3-7)
[c]From selling expenses budget (Exhibit 3-8)
[d]From general and administrative expenses budget (Exhibit 3-9)

In Sweet Temptations' cash budget, information came from the sales, purchases, selling expenses, and general and administrative expenses budgets. A service company's cash budget information, on the other hand, would be obtained from its sales budget and its operating expenses budget. Information from these budgets would be used in the same way that a retail company uses its information to prepare the projected financial statements we discuss in the next sections.

The Projected Income Statement

A **projected income statement** summarizes a company's expected revenues and expenses for the budget period, assuming the company follows its plans. Note that the projected income statement is *not* the same as the cash budget. In Exhibit 3-4, we showed the relationship between sales revenues from credit sales and cash collections from sales. If a company has credit sales, cash receipts occur later than the related sales. The same thing can happen with expenses. Many times, the cash payment for an expense occurs later than the activity that causes the expense. For example, usually employees work before being paid. If the work occurs late in March, the company may not pay the employees until early in April. The projected salaries expense will appear on the projected income statement for the quarter that ends in March (since the work occurred in March), but the projected cash payment will appear on April's cash budget. In other words, timing differences between the operating activities and the related cash receipts and payments cause the differences between the projected income statement and the cash budget. The projected income statement reports on the company's planned operating activities, whereas the cash budget reports on the expected cash receipts and payments related to those activities.

The projected income statement is important because it shows what the company's profit will be if the company follows its plans. At this point in the budgeting process, if the expected profit for the budget period is not satisfactory, the entrepreneur may revise the company's plans to try to increase the profit. In Chapter 2 we discussed how a company uses C-V-P analysis to estimate how some changes in plans will affect its profit. If, as a result of this analysis, the entrepreneur changes the company's plans, then the budgets are changed according to these revised plans.

 What changes do you think an entrepreneur might make in a company's plans to increase its expected profit?

Exhibit 3-11 shows Sweet Temptations' projected income statement for the first quarter of 2011. Sweet Temptations includes this income statement in its business plan. There are three differences between this statement and the income statement[1] for internal decision-makers that we showed in Exhibit 2-8. First, the income statement in Exhibit 3-11 is for the first *quarter* of 2011. To keep the discussion simple, we showed only the income statement for January in Exhibit 2-8. (If Sweet Temptations had chosen to show an income statement for each month of the first quarter in Exhibit 3-11, the January profits of Exhibits 3-11 and 2-8 would be identical.) Second, in Exhibit 3-11 we group the fixed costs into two categories—selling expenses and general and administrative expenses. In Exhibit 2-8 we listed each expense separately and did not attempt to categorize them. Finally, in Exhibit 3-11 we do not list all the separate expenses because they are shown in the selling expenses and general and administrative expenses budgets.

Notice that the amounts of most of the revenues and expenses in the projected income statement in Exhibit 3-11 come from the budgets we discussed earlier. The variable cost of boxes of candy sold, however, is computed by multiplying the budgeted number of boxes *sold* during the quarter (2,460, from the sales budget in Exhibit 3-5) by Sweet Temptations' cost per box ($4.50, from the purchases budget in Exhibit 3-7). So the cost of boxes of chocolates *sold* that Sweet Temptations listed on its projected income statement is different from the cost of boxes of chocolates *purchased* that Sweet Temptations listed on its purchase budget. This is because the number of boxes sold is different than the number of boxes purchased.

EXHIBIT 3-11	PROJECTED INCOME STATEMENT

SWEET TEMPTATIONS
Projected Income Statement
For the Quarter Ended March 31, 2011

Total sales revenue		$24,600[a]
Less total variable costs		
Cost of boxes of chocolates sold		(11,070)[b]
Total contribution margin		$13,530
Less total fixed costs:		
Selling expenses	$8,902.50[c]	
General and administrative expenses	2,647.50[d]	
Total fixed costs		(11,550)
Profit		$ 1,980

[a]From the sales budget (Exhibit 3-5).
[b]The 2,460 budgeted total sales in number of boxes (Exhibit 3-5) times the $4.50 cost per box (Exhibit 3-7).
[c]From the selling expenses budget (Exhibit 3-8).
[d]From the general and administrative expenses budget (Exhibit 3-9).

---

[1]We could rearrange this income statement so that it would look similar to the income statement for external users that we show in Exhibit 2-8. To save space, we do not include the rearranged income statement in Exhibit 3-11.

The Projected Balance Sheet

In Chapter 1, we indicated that a balance sheet is a basic financial statement of a company. A balance sheet shows a company's financial position on a particular date. It lists the company's assets, liabilities, and owner's equity. In the same way, a **projected balance sheet** summarizes a company's expected financial position at the end of a budget period, assuming the company follows its plans. Usually, a company includes a projected balance sheet in its master budget. Because preparing a projected balance sheet can be complex, we will wait until Chapter 11 to show one. If we did include a projected balance sheet for Sweet Temptations, it would show what resources (assets) Sweet Temptations expects to have, how much it expects to owe its creditors (liabilities), and what it expects Anna's investment (owner's equity) in the assets of the company to be at the end of the quarter.

USING THE MASTER BUDGET IN EVALUATING THE COMPANY'S PERFORMANCE

Managers of all types of companies use budgets as planning tools. Budgeting is also a valuable tool for *evaluating* how a company, division, department, or team actually performed. By analyzing differences between a company's budgeted results and its actual results, a manager can determine where plans went wrong and where to take corrective action next time.

6 How can a manager use a budget to evaluate a company's performance and then use the results of that evaluation to influence the company's plans?

Finding Differences between Actual and Budgeted Amounts

Comparing budgeted amounts to actual results is an important part of the budgeting process. By using the budgets discussed in this chapter as benchmarks, a manager can evaluate the differences between the actual performance of the company and its planned performance. By understanding *why* the differences occurred, a manager can decide what actions to take for future time periods. For example, Exhibit 3-12 shows a comparison (called a **cost report**) between Sweet Temptations' budgeted and actual expenses for the first quarter of 2011. A large company would usually divide its cost report into selling expenses and general and administrative expenses, and also by division, department, manager, product, or some other identifiable unit. This breakdown is not necessary for Sweet Temptations' cost report, because it has only a few items.

EXHIBIT 3-12	COMPARISON OF ACTUAL VS. BUDGETED AMOUNTS

SWEET TEMPTATIONS COMPANY
Cost Report
For the Quarter Ended March 31, 2011

	Budgeted	Actual	Favorable (Unfavorable) Difference
Rent expense	$ 3,000	$ 3,000	—
Salaries expense	6,150	6,150	—
Consulting expense	600	600	—
Advertising expense	915	915	—
Supplies expense	90	110	$(20)
Depreciation expense	45	45	—
Telephone and utilities expense	750	800	(50)
	$11,550	$11,620	$(70)

With a quick glance at this cost report, you can see that Sweet Temptations' actual expenses were $70 greater than budgeted expenses in the first quarter of 2011. You can even see that the negative difference between total planned and actual expenses occurs because the telephone and utilities expense as well as the supplies expense were more than expected. However, knowing that there are differences is not enough information for a manager to use in explaining the differences and in planning the next time period's activities. It is at this point in the evaluation process that a manager must use creative and critical thinking skills. A manager can learn about the causes of the differences by asking questions and investigating further. The cost report gives the manager a starting point from which to begin an investigation.

Learning Why Differences Occur

While analyzing the difference between the budgeted and the actual telephone and utility expense, Anna might ask herself questions such as the following:

1. Which of the monthly telephone and utility bills were higher or lower than expected?
2. Why were these bills different from what was expected? Was there a difference because Sweet Temptations has just begun operations and Anna had no previous experience to use in estimating what the expenses would be?
3. Did the difference occur because of selling activities or because of general and administrative activities (or both)?
4. What other explanations are there for the differences?

After formulating the questions she wants answered, Anna can devise a strategy to find the answers. Looking for answers will require Anna's creative thinking skills. Suppose she decides to start her investigation by first looking at the monthly telephone and utility bills. If she finds minor differences between planned and actual expenses for all the bills except for the electricity bill, these minor differences can be attributed to her use of estimates. Minor differences from estimates are to be expected, so there would be no need to plan any correcting activities for the future. Suppose, however, that in looking at the electricity bill, Anna discovers that the electric company raised its rate 10 percent since she created the budget. Before planning for the next quarter, Anna must ask another question: Will the same increase be in effect next quarter? If so, Anna will use this information in her future planning and budgeting activities, and the next master budget will include the 10 percent increase in Sweet Temptations' planned electricity expenses.

 What questions do you think Anna should ask about the difference between planned and actual supplies expenses?

A manager can use information from the master budget to help identify the causes of differences between budgeted and actual expenses, and then to decide what to change in the future. As you just saw, an analysis of the causes of these differences may lead an owner or manager to make changes in future budgets. On the other hand, the same analysis may lead the owner or manager to change future activities rather than future budgets. For example, suppose packaging workers at Unlimited Decadence are working overtime repackaging boxes of chocolates because of a sudden decrease in the quality of purchased packaging materials. Because of this unplanned problem, the actual salary expense for Unlimited Decadence will be higher than its budgeted salary expense. An analysis of the cause of this salary difference may lead the packaging manager to look for a new supplier of packaging materials.

Differences between planned and actual expenses can also be positive differences. For example, Sweet Temptations' telephone and utility expense could have been less than the budgeted expense. Suppose Anna based Sweet Temptations' budgeted telephone and

Do you think Burger King's estimate of Big King sales affected its estimate of sales of french fries?

utilities expense on a well-publicized planned increase in utility rates. If the state Public Utility Commission later turns down the rate increase, Sweet Temptations' actual expense will be less than the budgeted expense. Anna will use this rate information, which she noticed because of her analysis of the difference between the planned and the actual expenses, for her future planning activities. Unless circumstances change between this budget period and the next budget period, Anna will use the old rate to budget Sweet Temptations' utilities expense.

At other times, differences between planned and actual results can have both positive and negative consequences. Consider when **Burger King** first introduced its "Big King" sandwich as competition against **McDonald's** "Big Mac" sandwich. In its sales budget, Burger King had estimated that it would sell 1.8 million Big Kings a day. The good news was that the sandwich was so popular at that time that Burger King sold nearly 3 million per day—about 70 percent more than it had expected! The bad news was that since Burger King had budgeted and then made its purchases based on anticipated sales, the *un*anticipated sales quickly caused shortages in Big King sandwiches in many cities, causing Burger King to miss the additional sales.

BUSINESS ISSUES AND VALUES

The accounting information included in budgets affects and is affected by business decisions. In using this information for decision making, entrepreneurs must also consider other, nonfinancial issues. For example, suppose a small new airline has entered a market dominated by a large, well-established airline. To effectively compete, the new company determines that it must cut costs. A look at the budget shows that one of the largest costs, and an easy one to reduce, is maintenance costs on the fleet. When making the decision about whether to reduce maintenance costs, the entrepreneur would need to consider whether reducing these costs now would drive up future maintenance costs. But more importantly, the entrepreneur would need to consider the safety of the passengers and crew. In this case, the safety concern may outweigh the financial gain resulting from reducing the maintenance costs.

SUMMARY

At the beginning of the chapter we asked you several questions. During the chapter, we asked you to STOP and answer some additional questions to build your knowledge about specific issues. Be sure you answered these additional questions. Below are the questions from the beginning of the chapter, with a brief summary of the key points relating to the answers. Use your creative and critical thinking skills to expand on these key points to develop more complete answers to the questions and to determine what other questions you have that might lead you to learn more about the issues.

1   How does a budget contribute toward helping a company achieve its goals?

A budget helps a company by giving a financial description of the activities planned by the company to help it achieve its goals. It also helps by adding order to the planning process, by providing an opportunity to recognize and avoid potential operating problems, by quantifying plans, and by creating a "benchmark" for evaluating the company's performance.

2   Do the activities of a company have a logical order that influences the organization of a budget?

Yes, the operating activities of the company make up what is called the company's *operating cycle*. A company's operating cycle is the average time it takes the company to use cash to buy goods and services, to sell these goods to or perform services for customers, and to collect cash from these customers. The order of activities, and the cash receipts and payments associated with these activities, influence how a company organizes its budget.

3   What is the structure of the budgeting process, and how does a company begin that process?

The master budget is the overall structure used for the financial description of a company's plans. It consists of a set of budgets describing planned company activities, the cash receipts or payments that should result from these activities, and the company's projected financial statements (what the financial statements should look like if the planned activities occur). The budgeting process begins with the sales budget because product or service sales affect all other company activities. By gathering various types of information, such as past sales data, knowledge about customer needs, industry trends, economic forecasts, and new technological developments, a company estimates the amount of inventory (or employee time) to be sold in each budget period. Cash collections from sales are planned by examining the company's credit-granting policies. Cash payments for expenses are planned by examining the company's payment policies.

4   What are the similarities and differences between a retail company's master budget and a service company's master budget?

For a retail company, the master budget usually includes a sales budget, a purchases budget, a selling expenses budget, a general and administrative expenses budget, a cash budget, a projected income statement, and a projected balance sheet. A service company does not have a purchases budget, and it usually has one operating expenses budget.

5   After a company begins the budgeting process, is there a strategy it can use to complete the budget?

Yes. For example, a retail company follows a strategy similar to the following. After budgeting sales, the company plans the amount and timing of inventory purchases. To budget purchases, the company examines the costs associated with inventory purchases and storage as well as the costs of not carrying enough inventory. It also considers its policy on required inventory levels. After budgeting purchases, the company plans the cash payments for inventory purchases by reviewing its payment agreements with suppliers. To budget expenses, the company must first determine the behaviors of these expenses. It budgets fixed expenses by evaluating previous fixed expenses and then adjusting them (if necessary) according to the plans for the coming time period. It budgets variable expenses by first observing what activity causes these expenses to vary and then computing the total expenses by multiplying the cost per unit of activity by the budgeted activity level. For a retail company, the activity level is usually sales. The company budgets the cash payments for these expenses by reviewing the company's policy on the payment of expenses. The information for developing the cash budget comes from the other previously prepared budgets, as does the information for creating the projected income statement.

⑥ How can a manager use a budget to evaluate a company's performance and then use the results of that evaluation to influence the company's plans?

A manager uses a master budget to evaluate a company's performance by comparing the information in the various budgets with the results that occur after the planned activities are implemented. The manager identifies the differences between budgeted and actual results, and learns about the causes of these differences by asking questions and investigating further. Based on these investigations, a manager may adjust the company's activities and plans, as well as its future budgets.

KEY TERMS

budget *(p. 73)*
budgeting *(p. 73)*
cash budget *(p. 87)*
cost report *(p. 91)*
financing activities section *(p. 88)*
general and administrative expenses
 budget *(p. 85)*
investing activities section *(p. 88)*
management by exception *(p. 74)*
master budget *(p. 76)*

operating activities section *(p. 88)*
projected balance sheet *(p. 91)*
projected income statement *(p. 89)*
purchases budget *(p. 82)*
retail company's operating cycle *(p. 74)*
sales budget *(p. 78)*
selling expenses budget *(p. 84)*
service company's operating cycle
 (p. 75)

SUMMARY SURFING

Here is an opportunity to gather information on the Internet about real-world issues related to the topics in this chapter (for suggestions on how to navigate various organizations' Web sites to find the relevant information, see the related discussion in the Preface at the beginning of the book). Answer the following questions.

- Go to the **Canada Business Online Small Business Workshop** Web site. What is a cash flow forecast, and how does it compare with the cash budget that we discussed in the chapter? What are the steps involved in preparing a cash flow forecast? How would preparing the budgets discussed in the chapter help an entrepreneur in preparing a cash flow forecast?

- Go to the **Entrepreneur.com** Web site. How often should a company update its business plan? What are the benefits to a company of keeping its business plan current?

INTEGRATED BUSINESS AND ACCOUNTING SITUATIONS

Answer the Following Questions in Your Own Words.

Testing Your Knowledge

3-1 What is it about budgeting that adds discipline to the planning process?

3-2 If a problem comes to light during the budgeting process, what is the manager likely to do?

3-3   "Budgeting serves as a benchmark for evaluation." Explain what that means.

3-4   Describe a master budget. Why might a master budget be different from one company to another?

3-5   How are the master budgets of a retail company and a service company similar to each other? How are they different from each other?

3-6   Describe the operating cycle of a retail company. How are the operating cycles of a retail company and a service company similar to and different from each other?

3-7   Why must the sales budget be developed before any of the other budgets? Where does information for sales forecasts come from?

3-8   If you just finished budgeting sales for next year, what information would you need to be able to budget cash collections from sales?

3-9   How does knowing forecasted sales help a manager develop a purchases budget? What else besides forecasted sales would a manager have to know to complete the purchases budget?

3-10   When developing a selling expenses budget and a general and administrative expenses budget, why do you have to know how expenses behave?

3-11   Why must you complete all the other budgets before you can develop the cash budget?

3-12   Why is it important to know about anticipated cash shortages ahead of time?

3-13   What is a "cash buffer" and what is an example of a circumstance where a company could use one?

3-14   Why is having too much cash on hand a problem?

3-15   On the cash budget, why is the beginning cash balance for January the same as the beginning cash balance for the first quarter of the year? Why is the March ending cash balance the same as the first quarter's ending cash balance? How do you determine the first quarter's cash receipts from sales?

3-16   How is the cash budget similar to a cash flow statement? How are they different from each other?

3-17   Why is the cash budget not the same as the projected income statement? What items included on the projected income statement are not included on the cash budget?

3-18   In evaluating a company's performance, why do managers or owners need to learn the causes of differences between actual and budgeted amounts?

Applying Your Knowledge

3-19   Jaime's Hat Shop sells hats with college logos on them; the hats sell for $22 each. This year, Jaime's expects to sell 350 hats in May, 300 in June, 400 in July, 800 in August, 1,040 in September, and 750 in October. On average, 25 percent of its customers purchase on credit. Jaime's allows those customers to pay for their purchases the month after they have made their purchases.

Required: Prepare a sales budget for Jaime's Hat Shop for the third quarter of this year.

3-20   Refer to 3-19. Company policy is to plan to end each month with an ending inventory equal to 20 percent of the next month's projected sales. Jaime's pays $8 for each hat that it purchases. Jaime and his supplier have an arrangement that allows Jaime's Hat Shop to pay for each purchase 60 days after the purchase.

Required: Prepare a purchases budget for the third quarter of this year for Jaime's Hat Shop.

3-21   Refer to 3-19. Jaime's ended the second quarter of this year with 60 hats on hand.

Required: (1) Notice that Jaime's ended the second quarter with less than 20 percent of projected sales for July. What do you think accounts for the difference?

(2) How many hats should Jaime's purchase in July?

3-22 Refer to 3-19. Jaime's Hat Shop expects to incur the following expenses for each month of the third quarter of this year:

Rent (30% general and administrative, 70% selling)	$1,200
Utilities (30% general and administrative, 70% selling)	600
Advertising	400
Salaries (50% general and administrative, 50% selling)	5,000
Commissions (for each hat sold)	2

In January, Jaime's had prepaid the rent for the whole year. Jaime plans to pay for all the other expenses in the month they occur.

Required: (1) Prepare a selling expenses budget for the third quarter of this year.

(2) Prepare a general and administrative expenses budget for the third quarter of this year.

3-23 Refer to 3-19 through 3-22. Jaime's Hat Shop ended June with a cash balance of $10,343.

Required: Prepare a cash budget for the third quarter of this year.

3-24 Refer to 3-19 through 3-22.

Required: Prepare a projected income statement for the third quarter of this year.

3-25 Mark and Lawanda are partners in a new executive search company called Executive Lost and Found. Executive Lost and Found, which begins operations in December, matches the skills of displaced executives (executives who have been laid off) with the needs of companies looking for top managers. Mark estimates that the employees of Executive Lost and Found will spend 1,000 hours in December, 1,400 hours in January, 1,600 hours in February, and 1,450 hours in March working on filling executive positions for Lost and Found's clients. Executive Lost and Found will bill each of its clients at the end of the month, charging $400 per hour spent working for that client during the month. On average, 50% of the billings for any month will be collected during the following month, 30% during the second month following the billing, and 20% during the third month following the billing.

Required: Prepare a sales budget for Executive Lost and Found for the quarter (January through March).

3-26 Butler Company sells a single product for $6 per unit. Sales estimates (in units) for the last four months of the year are as follows:

	Units
September	40,000
October	45,000
November	35,000
December	40,000

All of Butler's sales are credit sales, and it expects to collect each account receivable 15 days after the related sale. Assume that all months have 30 days.

Required: Prepare a sales budget for the last three months of the year, including estimated collections of accounts receivable.

3-27 The sales budget for Merita Medallion Company shows budgeted sales (in medallions) for December and the first four months of next year:

	Medallions
December	100,000
January	40,000
February	90,000
March	150,000
April	50,000

Required: Prepare a budget for the number of medallions Merita needs to purchase in the first three months of next year for each of the following two *independent* situations:

(1) The company's policy is to have inventory on hand at the end of each month equal to 15% of the following month's sales requirement.

(2) The company's policy is to keep each month's ending inventory to a minimum without letting it fall below 5,000 medallions. Assume that the December 1 inventory has 5,000 medallions and that the company's only supplier is willing to sell a maximum of 125,000 medallions to the company per month.

3-28   Top Dog Pet Store sells dog food in 20-pound bags for $10 per bag, which it buys from its supplier for $7 per bag. Top Dog estimates that its sales of bags of dog food for the second quarter of the year will be as follows:

	Bags
April	1,200
May	1,400
June	1,500

Top Dog's policy is to have bags of dog food on hand at the end of each month equal to 10% of the next month's budgeted sales (bags). It expects to have 120 bags of dog food on hand at the end of March and expects to sell 1,650 bags in July. Top Dog expects its cost of purchases to be $7,770 in March; it pays for its purchases in the following month.

Required: (1) Prepare a purchases budget for bags of dog food for the second quarter of this year for Top Dog.

(2) How many bags of dog food did Top Dog expect to sell in March?

3-29   Blanchar Business Machines estimates its monthly selling expenses as follows:

Advertising	$22,000 per month
Sales salaries	$18,000 per month
Sales calls on customers	$35 per machine
Commissions paid to sales personnel	$50 per machine
Delivery	$20 per machine

Assume that Blanchar pays selling expenses in the month after they are incurred. Based on current plans of Blanchar's sales department, monthly sales estimates are as follows: March—80 units, April—90 units, May—100 units, June—120 units.

Required: Prepare a selling expense budget for the *second* quarter for Blanchar Business Machines.

3-30   That Fat Cat Company sells cat food in ten-pound bags for $6.20 per bag. Sales estimates for the first three months of the year are as follows:

	Bags
January	40,000
February	35,000
March	30,000

December sales were 30,000 bags of cat food. That Fat Cat's desired ending inventory of cat food each month is 30% of the next month's sales estimate (in bags). All sales are cash sales. That Fat Cat purchases bags of cat food at $4.70 per bag and pays for them the month *after* the purchase. General and administrative expenses total $35,000 per month (including $20,000 depreciation), and That Fat Cat pays for these expenses (except for depreciation) in the same month they are incurred. January's current liabilities (all to be paid in January) total $71,500. The company's cash balance on January 1 is $75,000.

Required: Prepare a cash budget for each of the first two months of the year.

3-31   Refer to 3-30.

Required: Prepare a projected income statement for February. How do you explain the differences between the income statement and the cash budget?

3-32 Suppose you are a banker, and the controller of a small company asks you for a short-term $10,000 loan, due in 120 days. Interest on the loan would be 12%, due when the loan is paid back. To support his request, he gives you the following information from his company's cash budget for the next quarter:

	January	February	March	Quarter
Cash flow from operations:				
Cash receipts from sales	$20,000	$14,400	$13,600	$48,000
Cash payments for				
Purchases	$15,000	$10,800	$10,200	$36,000
Selling expenses	3,300	3,300	3,300	9,900
General and administrative expenses	1,650	650	650	2,950
Total payments	$19,950	$14,750	$14,150	$48,850
Net cash inflow (outflow) from operations	$ 50	$ (350)	$ (550)	$ (850)
Cash flow from investments:				
Cash receipt from sale of equipment		3,000		3,000
Net cash inflow (outflow) from operations and investments	$ 50	$ 2,650	$ (550)	$ 2,150
Add: Beginning cash balance	4,880	4,930	7,580	4,880
Ending cash balance from operations and investments	$ 4,930	$ 7,580	$ 7,030	$ 7,030

Required: (1) What is your first reaction?

(2) Before making your decision, what else would you like to know about this company? Can any of what you would like to know be found in any of the company's other budgets or financial statements? What other budgets or statements would you like the owner to provide for you? What information would you hope to get from each of these budgets or statements?

(3) What other information would help you make your decision?

(4) Can you think of any circumstances in which it would be a good idea to loan this company $10,000?

(5) Depending on the information you are able to get, what other alternatives are there to loaning or not loaning this company $10,000?

3-33 Joe, Billy, Ray, and Bob are business partners who own Joe Billy Ray Bob's Country and Western Wear. Joe Billy Ray Bob's arrangement with all of its clothing suppliers allows it to pay for its merchandise purchases one month after the purchases have been made. About 15% of their customers make purchases on credit. These customers pay for their purchases one month after they have made their purchases. All the partners agree that a bank loan would allow Joe Billy Ray Bob's to revamp the storefront (perhaps causing more customers to want to come inside and shop). The partners are having a disagreement, however, about the cash budget that they plan to include in their loan application package. Joe, Billy, and Bob believe that the budget should be revised to present the bank with the most positive projected cash flows. To accomplish this revision, they are suggesting that on the cash budget, payments for purchases be shown *two* months after the purchases have been made, rather than one month as agreed to by Joe Billy Ray Bob's suppliers. Joe, Billy, and Bob are also suggesting that cash receipts from credit customers be budgeted in the same month as the related sales rather than one month later, even though they expect these customers to wait a month before paying for their purchases. Ray thinks the budget should reflect the partners' actual expectations. The partners have come to you for advice.

Required: (1) What ethical issues are involved in this decision?

(2) If the partners make the revisions, what effect will the revisions have on the sales budget? on the purchases budget? on the cash budget?

(3) Who stands to gain and who stands to lose by this budget revision? Is the gain or loss temporary or permanent, short-term or long-term?

(4) How might the bank be hurt by the changed budget? How might the company be hurt by the changed budget?

(5) Since the budget represents a plan of action, how might the changed budget affect the activities of the company during the budget period?

(6) Are there other alternatives to choose from besides changing the budget or not changing the budget?

(7) What do you recommend that the partners do?

3-34   Assume that a company collects two-thirds of its sales revenue in the month of sale and the remaining one-third in the following month.

Required: How much revenue has the company actually earned in the month of the sale? Should the company record revenue on the income statement in the month when it collects the cash or when the work was done to earn the revenue? What reasons do you have for choosing one alternative over the other? (What are your reasons for not choosing the other alternative?)

3-35   The airline industry is very competitive—management is under constant pressure to improve company profits. Ideas that could improve profits include the following:

(a) Increasing the price of tickets
(b) Reducing the number of flight attendants
(c) Reducing the number of flights on which meals are served
(d) Serving smaller meals or serving snacks instead of meals
(e) Limiting the size of—or eliminating—raises
(f) Reducing the number of baggage handlers
(g) Charging a fee for extra checked bags
(h) Charging an extra fee for exit row seats

Required: For each of these ideas, describe the effect the idea would have on each of the budgets and on the projected financial statements. What other issues should management consider in deciding whether to implement any of these ideas?

3-36   Bill Morgan is the manager of the sales department of Rise & Shine Company, which sells deluxe bread makers. At the beginning of each month, Bill estimates the total cost of operating the department for the month. At the end of the month he compares the total estimated costs to the total actual costs to determine the difference. If the difference is "small," he doesn't investigate any further because he prefers to spend his time on "more important" issues.

At the beginning of April, Bill estimated that the total operating costs of the sales department would be $60,500. For April, the actual operating costs were $60,400. At the end of April, Bill says, "The sales department is doing pretty well. We came in $100 under budget for the month."

Alice Hoch, the president of the company, has come to you for help. She says, "I am concerned that we are not doing enough analysis of our costs, and I need your help. Start with the sales department and prepare for me a cost report to help me review the costs for April. You can have whatever information you need."

Upon investigation, you find the sales department was expected to sell 500 units (bread makers) in April. Based on these projected sales, its budgeted fixed costs were as follows: advertising, $18,000 and salaries, $25,000, while its budgeted variable costs were $25 commission per unit sold and $10 delivery cost per unit sold. You determine that, during April, 500 units were sold and the sales department spent $19,300 for advertising and $22,600 for salaries. It also paid the $25 commission per unit sold and paid $6,000 for delivering the 500 units.

Required: Write a report to the president that (a) includes a cost report for the sales department that compares the budgeted costs to the actual costs for April, (b) identifies the questions you think the president should ask to analyze any differences you find, and (c) suggests some potential answers to the questions.

3-37   Joe Collagen is the president of a small retail company that sells a skin-smoothing lotion and that has been operating for several years. He keeps meticulous records of his actual operating activities, including monthly sales, purchases, and operating expenses, as well as the related cash receipts and payments. However, Joe has never prepared a master budget for the company. He comes to you for help and says, "My profits have been slowly decreasing and I don't know why. Also, sometimes when I least expect it, the company runs short of cash and I have to invest more into it. I've heard that preparing a master budget is a good thing to do, but I don't know what is involved or where to begin."

Required: Prepare a report to the president that (a) explains what budgets and projected financial statements are included in a master budget, and (b) clearly specifies how he would use the information from his previous actual operating activities to develop each of these budgets and the projected income statement.

3-38 Steve and Tammy are thinking of opening a fitness center with facilities for aerobics, weight training, jogging, and lap swimming as well as diet and injury consultation. They plan to buy land and build their facility near the new shopping mall. They want to employ a director, an assistant director, experts to supervise members in each fitness area, and numerous consulting dietitians and sports medicine professionals. They hope to have the entire facility, including an outdoor all-weather track and an indoor swimming pool, completed by the end of the year. They also believe that it will be important to have the facility fully equipped and staffed before they begin taking memberships. Although their estimates indicate that the fitness center can be profitable if they can establish a growing membership over the first five or six years, many small businesses in town have failed because of "cash flow problems" (excess of cash payments over cash receipts). Before committing themselves to this venture, Steve and Tammy have come to you for advice and for help in preparing a cash budget.

Required: Write Steve and Tammy a memo explaining why they might have cash flow problems during their early periods of operations. Show them how they can identify these cash flow problems through careful cash budgeting. Make a few suggestions that might help them reduce such problems if they do decide to open the fitness center.

3-39 Yesterday, you received the following letter for your advice column in the local paper:

DR. DECISIVE

Dear Dr. Decisive:

Please help my overly compulsive girlfriend, who even reads your column compulsively. She is on the New Housing Committee of her sorority. (They are planning to build a new house.) Last night, after a great movie, she was telling me that her sorority had to take a budget to the bank in order to get a loan. Then she told me about their budget, and I can't BELIEVE how "nitpicky" it is—and I told her so in those words. Well, the movie was terrific, but the evening turned out to be a disaster. We got into a MAJOR fight, and now she says she doesn't want to go out with me next weekend (not that I want to go out with someone so COMPULSIVE next weekend). Here are the details of what I told her:

1. It doesn't matter that her sorority has a problem collecting dues and rent from its members. The members always pay eventually, and that's all the bank needs to know.

2. It doesn't matter that the electric company plans to raise the utility rate it charges. That's the future—

this is now. Her sorority should budget costs that are real (costs they have already experienced), not costs based on the plans of the electric company.

Please explain to her why you agree with me and why these issues will not affect the bank's decision. Maybe she will realize that her compulsion is EXTREME and then we will be able to go out next weekend. I'm just

"Laid Back."

Required: Meet with your Dr. Decisive team and write a response to "Laid Back."

ENDNOTES

[a]http://www.webmd.com/diet/news/20030827/dark-chocolate-is-healthy-chocolate; http://www.reuters.com/article/pressRelease/idUS159307+30-Jul-2008+BW20080730.

[b]http://www.dailymail.co.uk/health/diets/article-1031694/Bitter-sweet-Dark-chocolate-sales-double-years.html